ISRAEL
from the AIR

WHITE STAR
PUBLISHERS

ISRAEL *from the* AIR

Photographs
Itamar Grinberg

Texts
David Kriss

Graphic design
Anna Galliani

CONTENTS

© 1998 White Star S.r.l.
Via C. Sassone 22/24
13100 Vercelli, Italy

ISBN 88-8095-319-2

Printed in 1998 by
Grafiche Mazzucchelli, Milan.
Color separation Grafiche
Mazzucchelli, Milan.

1 Agriculture has been central to the taming of the Land and the forging of its people.

2-3 The Old City of Jerusalem with the Judean Desert in the background. The last rays of sunlight reflecting off the golden Dome of the Rock illuminate the area with a warm glow. Within Jerusalem's 16th century city walls, built by Suleiman the Magnificent, lie monuments recalling events that forged and cradled mankind's three monotheistic religions.

4-5 Advanced agricultural technology, a warm climate and years of work have allowed formerly barren areas, like the Jordan Valley to green and bloom. The Jordan Valley, part of the Syrian-African Rift runs down Israel's eastern flank.

6-7 Masada, Herod's solitary citadel, juts out into the Judean Desert and commands the Dead Sea. The determination of Masada's Jewish zealot defenders to die by their own hand rather than be killed by the Romans, has become a potent symbol for modern Israel.

8 Tel Aviv, the first Jewish city, is Israel's cultural and commercial capital and the heart of its main urban conurbation. Hung above a busy intersection, Dizengoff Circle, a Tel Aviv symbol, now contains a sculpture spouting fire and water created by Israeli artist Ya'akov Agam.

9 On the Temple Mount or Haram al Sharif, sites central to Judaism and Islam co-exist in close proximity. The magnificent golden Dome of the Rock seems to preside over the area. In the lower right foreground, thousands of Jewish worshippers pray at the sacred Western Wall, one of the retaining walls of the Second Temple compound.

ɴTRODUCTION

by DAVID KRISS

I srael can be considerd as a dot on the globe that altered the course of mankind more than any other land on earth. The Israel so defined is the "Promised Land" of the patriarchs, the Holy Land of priests and prophets, the Terra Sancta on which three religions adopted the all–embracing idea of One God, the soil on which they nourished their traditions and where the epic stories of their faith unfolded.

Or perhaps we should talk about The Land of Israel that was later known as Palestine; that ancient semitic pathway, a strategic target for empire builders, each leaving its mark on the land in layer after layer of civilisation, each signifying conquest and defeat in sobering succession.

But what about the Israel that has gathered together its people from a hundred lands in what could be described as a dream of nationhood come true.
The Israel that was the focal point to which the Jewish people prayed for two millennia and where its old–new Hebrew language is taught by native–born Israeli children to their immigrant parents.

This Israel is the "State of Israel" the bustling young modern democracy, established in 1948, a world leader in information technology, a country restlessly,

and sometimes painfully, struggling to define its own identity and its place in the Middle East and the Mediterranean Basin.

In Israel the modern and the ancient, the sacred and the secular, the visionary and the prosaic bump and collide in a jostling mosaic that can overwhelm the senses and defy the imagination.

Traversed by both the camel and the supersonic jet, Israel is where West meets East in a magnificent confusion of local and transplanted cultures that somehow combine to make sense.

And then there is the Land itself. For all who live on it, the land has a significance bordering on the religious, even for the majority of Israelis who do not define themselves as religious.

Consciousness of the Land and all it implies has even permeated the language.

Israelis are as likely to use the word "Ha–aretz"—The Land—as they are "Israel". "Love of the Land" and "Knowledge of the Land" have become national credos.

10 At the southern tip of the Sea of Galilee the River Jordan meanders amid lush fields flanked by the agricultural settlements of Kinneret and Degania Aleph, the first communal farm and the "Mother of Kibbutzim".

11 Citrus orchards in the Sharon area. For many years citrus fruits were one of the mainstays of Israel's fledgling economy.

And like the people who live upon it, the physical landscape is varied and full of clashes and contrasts. As if the Creator had decided to place all his toys in one small corner, He blessed Israel with a Mediterranean shoreline, a searing Rift Valley, rich verdant fields, expanses of arid desert, coral reefs and even snow–capped peaks. On the ground, the geographical and climatic changes can be dramatic. For example, the more adventurous could be skiing on Mount Hermon in the morning and basking in sub–tropical temperatures of the Sea of Galilee in the afternoon. Laid out from above like a relief map, Israel's topography provides the explanation for these exhilarating shifts.

The northern half of this long and narrow country can be roughly divided into three longitudinal strips. From west to east, the first is the coastal plain that runs parallel to the Mediterranean and comprises of a sandy shoreline bordered by stretches of fertile farmland extending up to 25 miles inland.

The second strip is the central mountain range. This starts in the north as the Galilee hills and continues as the hills of Samaria and Judea lined with ancient terraced fields. The central mountain range is cut in half by the fertile Jezreel Valley.

Finally, there is the Jordan Valley, which in fact runs the entire eastern length of the country. This is a section

of the Syrian–African Rift, the great fissure split the earth's crust millions of years ago and extends from Syria to the Zambezi River in Africa. In the Galilee, this deep valley is bounded on the east by the Golan Heights. Israel's arid south—The Negev—comprises about half of the country's land area. Characterized by rolling hills in the north and peaks, craters and plateaus in its south, the Negev and the Arava (the southern extension of the Jordan Valley) lead into the Red Sea at Israel's southern tip.

Situated at the junction of Europe, Asia and Africa, Israel is bordered by Lebanon to the north, Syria to the northeast, Jordan to the east, Egypt to the southwest and

the Mediterranean Sea to the west. It is 290 miles in length and 85 miles across at its widest point. The width of the country, from the Mediterranean in the west to the Dead Sea in the east can be covered by car in about 90 minutes but it takes about eight hours to cover the northsouth trip from Metullah to Eilat.

We are in no hurry as we wend our way down the Land from above, zigzagging from north to south to wonder at its marvels and harden to its manifold tales.

Let us begin by swooping down from the highest mountain in the Near East. Mount Hermon rises to 9,200 feet and leads into the Golan Heights. Formed by volcanic eruptions, their steep cliffs glistening with fast mountain streams and concealing rocky pools, the Golan Heights rise to a broad basalt plateau. Their strategic importance is obvious.

At the crest of the cliffs, the green fields of the Hula Valley and the sparkling waters of the Sea of Galilee are laid out below.

Were it not for the fact that they are situated in the east, the Golan Heights could be considered Israel's "Wild West". The rugged terrain has an air of frontier country, heightened by the sight of cowboys driving their herds across the pastureland. Delicate mountain gazelle can also be seen springing over the slopes. In recent years the Golan has also proved to be excellent grape–growing country and this has produced a flourishing wine industry centered in the new town of Katzerin.

The Golan Heights were captured from Syria in the 1967 war and are presently occupied by Israel, which has established settlements on them. All or part of the Golan Heights could be returned to Syria in the framework of a peace agreement between Israel and Syria.

12-13 The snowcapped peaks of Mount Hermon on the Golan Heights. Nestling in the foothills are the village of Neve Ativ and the Druse town of Majd el Shams.

13 top In a tuck in the mountains at the southern extremity of the Golan Heights, Hamat Gader, with its hot mineral springs, has been a health spa since antiquity. Today it is equally famous for its alligator farm.

13 bottom Reservoirs in the northern plateau of Golan Heights. The Golan with its relatively high rainfall is a rich source of water. At springtime Mount Hermon's meltwater swells the sources of the River Jordan.

Israel is a new nation, but the collective memory of the Jewish people carries with it a two–thousand–year history of persecution in the diaspora. The new state's founders, seeking inspiration for a heroic national ethos, tended to hark back, not to the suffering of the more recent past but to the glorious battles of earlier periods of Jewish nationhood and pride. One such symbol of a valiant past is the Golan Heights stronghold of Gamla (from "camel"). This was the strategic site of a brave stand by Jewish zealots in the Great Revolt against Rome. After a bitter, month–long siege, the legions of the

Roman general Vespasian breached the defenses in A.D. 67. The defenders, rather than be taken captive, jumped to their deaths into the gorge below. This example of ultimate devotion to a cause has entered the iconology of modern Israel. The remains of a synagogue from this period, one of the many to be found on the Golan, bears witness. Now, in the nearby Gamla nature reserve, eagles glide effortlessly up and down the mountain ravines carried by warm air currents. It is fairly common to see birds of prey up here in the open spaces of the Golan and the Upper Galilee. An eagle, vulture or falcon soaring high above seems to look down with disdain upon the mere deeds of man.

Back on the slopes of Mount Hermon, the eagles can probably also spot skiers flashing down the slopes at the Neve Ativ ski resort. For four months of the year the crest of ("Grandfather") Hermon is covered with snow and from afar can resemble a white beard sticking into the sky. The battles for control of the strategic military position at its peak cost the lives of many Israeli and Syrian soldiers in the wars of 1967 and 1973. Nearby we come to the foreboding remains of Nimrod's Citadel (Kla'at Nimrod) perched on a rocky outcrop with a breathtaking view of the Golan and the Hulah Valley. Built by Muslim forces, it was conquered by the Crusaders in 1129 but was eventually retaken.

It is from this eagle's nest in the highlands that we can also savor our first bird's–eye view of the green hills and valleys of the Upper Galilee.

Twinkling in the distance are the streams that are the main sources of the River Jordan: the Banias, Dan and Snir. In the Upper Galilee, the River Jordan is still a gushing, tumbling torrent fed by melted snow from the foothills of Mount Hermon and the hills of Lebanon. From here it starts its long journey down eastern Israel via the Sea of Galilee until it reaches its final destination—the Dead Sea.

The upper courses of the River Jordan are a popular recreation area, where, according to the lay of the land, you can navigate whitewater rapids in an inflatable dinghy or canoe lazily along lush, willow–lined banks. Indeed, the entire north–east corner of the Upper Galilee is revealed as an enchanting land of springs and streams. The little paradise called Banias in Arabic, or Ein Panyas in Hebrew, is named after the god Pan.

This is an area of pools and waterfalls, climbing vines and stream foliage. It was an ancient cultic site and contains later shrines sacred to Druze and Muslims as well as the remains of a palace built by King Herod the Great and a Crusader city. Nearby Tel Dan is named after the Israelite tribe of Dan that occupied the previous Canaanite site in the twelfth century B.C. The fertility of the area around Dan is mentioned in the Bible: "For we have seen the Land, and behold, it is very good." (Judges 18:9). An Israelite city gate complex has been exposed here in archaeological excavations.

But for most visitors Dan is a cool and shady wonderland of streams and bridges, rich foliage and lush forests.

14 top Perched on top of the cliffs of the Onn nature reserve in the southern Golan, the kibbutz of Mevo Hama enjoys a magnificent view of the Sea of Galilee below. In the summer, these green hillsides quickly turn to yellow.

14 bottom In the south of the Golan Plateau next to the Hispin reservoir, lies the

moshav, or cooperative village, of Ramat Magshimim.

15 The camel-humped back of Gamla in the central Golan was once a city of Jewish Zealots who, as vividly described by the Jewish-Roman historian Josephus Flavius, committed collective suicide in the Great Revolt against the Romans.

16 top Founded at the end of the ninenth century, Metulla, on the Lebanese border, is Israel's northernmost town. The snowy peak on the horizon is Mount Hermon.

16 bottom In Israel's 1948 War of Independence, the defenders of the western Galilee kibbutz of Yehiam used the adjacent Judin Crusader Fortress for protection.

16-17 Montfort, in the western Galilee, was first erected by French Crusaders as a waystation for their pilgrims but was sold, in 1220, to the Teutonic Order, who turned it into a castle from which it ruled over the surrounding villages.

Banias and Tel Dan are just two of the more than 150 nature reserves dotted throughout the country that since 1964 have protected entire ecosystems and provided green lungs for harassed city dwellers. Hiking is an Israeli national pastime and on weekends and holidays many Israelis can be seen setting out to the countryside with a backpack and a sturdy pair of sandals (or a van full of elaborate camping gear) to reconnect with nature and feel the Land under their feet.

The Nature Reserve Authority together with the green organisations in Israel are fighting to balance development with protection of the environment. Israel's green lungs are under threat as the needs of a rising population take their toll.

Many of the formative events of Israel's pre–state pioneering period took place in the Galilee and these have become part of a national lore. For example, near Metullah, Israel's northernmost town, is Tel Hai, which contains a monument to one of Israel's heroic icons, the one–armed Josef Trumpeldor. Fatally wounded by Arab attackers in 1920, Trumpeldor was reputed to have uttered as his dying words, "It is good to die for one's country." While still in Russia, Trumpeldor was one of the founders of the He–Halutz (The Pioneer) youth movement which promoted "aliyah" (immigration: literally "ascending') to the Land of Israel and the establishment of a Zionist–Socialist center there. One of the movement's central ideas was that of "self–fulfilment" to be attained by means of devotion to this cause. After Trumpeldor's death The Josef Trumpeldor Labor Battalion was formed to build the land by establishing a commune of Jewish laborers to pave roads and build settlements and provide security. Ha–Shomer ("The Watchmen"), founded in 1908, was another organization, centered in the Galilee, that combined agricultural labor and defense. Dressed in Arab garb, members established and defended settlements and promoted the ideas of resourcefulness, courage and the use of weapons "only as a last resort." Such ideals (not always put into practice) were handed down to their successors, the Haganah and the Palmach, which fought from the 1920's through to the 1948 War of Independence and finally to the Israel Defense Forces, established after the creation of the State of Israel.

The swampy Hulah Valley to the south of Tel Hai is a further symbol of the Zionist pioneering spirit but also of how times have changed. The Hulah Lake was largely drained by pioneers in the early 1950's in order to rid

the area of malaria and to reclaim what they imagined would be fertile land. With malaria defeated and the land turning out to be less fertile than hoped, it is now being reflooded.

The last remnant of natural swampland in Israel, the Hulah Valley is the natural habitat of hundreds of species of fauna from water buffalo to huge flocks of pelicans and cranes stopping off on their migratory route to Africa.

Winging westwards, we enter the hill country that covers most of the Galilee. Much of it is forested with some of the 200 million trees that have been planted throughout Israel. The Upper Galilee is also dotted with the white–domed tombs of sheikhs and of venerated rabbis who were perhaps drawn to its wide vistas for inspiration and to its protected hilltop towns for defense.

Many of the rabbis, tombs are visited by devout Jews who believe that saying a prayer or lighting a candle in the hallowed proximity of a great rabbi will help them find a cure or a spouse. In the center of the Upper Galilee we find a town that more than any other in this region is associated with spirituality. Safed, perched on top of Mount Cana'an, was once a focal point for Jewish learning and, together with Jerusalem, Tiberias and Hebron is, in Jewish tradition, one of the four Sacred Cities of the Holy Land. Safed saw a flowering of Cabbalah (Jewish mysticism) in the sixtenth century when its Jewish population, swelled by immigrants expelled from Spain, made it the largest Jewish town in the country. Illustrious teachers of Jewish Law, poets and cabalists gathered to transform Safed into an important center for teaching, learning and the arcane practice of mysticism. At that time the Galilee was an important population center and Safed's silk and wool fabrics were renowned throughout Europe.

Safed's clear light, spiritual mountain setting and quaint old alleyways have also attracted many artists and today's visitors come for its old synagogues and art galleries. The town also hosts an annual festival of "klezmer" (traditional Jewish) music.

Meron, also near Safed, is where Rabbi Shimon bar Yochai is thought to have written his great cabalistic work—The Zohar.

His grave, visited by pilgrims throughout the year, is the site of ecstatic traditional annual celebrations attended by hundreds of thousands. Rising above it, Mount Meron, often covered in a mantle of mist, is the tallest mountain in Israel (over 3,600 feet) and is rich in natural woodland. On a clear day the observatory on its summit provides a wonderful view of the whole of the Galilee and, to the north, the hills of southern Lebanon.

The development of the modern Galilee and the transformation of its Jewish population from a religious community relying largely on charity to pioneering farmers might be traced back to 1878.

It was in that year that 150 residents of Safed, influenced by the new ideas emerging amongst the Jewish communities in Europe, descended Mount Cana'an to found Rosh Pina the first modern Jewish agricultural settlement in the Galilee. Rosh Pina became one of the early "moshavot."

These were villages that attempted, with the help of European philanthropists like Moses Montefiore and the Baron de Rothschild, to create the basis for a more self–sufficient, agricultural economy for the Jews of what was then Turkish–Ottoman controlled Palestine.

The year 1881 was another turning point, for it was then that the first wave of mainly Russian Jews, af-

18 The Carmel mountain range on the outskirts of Haifa is a nature reserve where the natural Mediterranean forest cover of oak and pine has been conserved.

18-19 A moshav in the Sharon area of the coastal plane produces flowers and vegetables in carefully controlled environments alongside open fields and orchards.

fected by the pogroms of that year and the reawakening of Jewish nationalism, began arriving in the country.

Formed into pioneering groups called Hovevei Zion (Lovers of Zion), they built up the new moshavot in such places as Rosh Pina, Yesud HaMa'ala and Metullah in the Galilee and Gedera, Ekron, Petah Tikva and Rishon Le–Zion in the center of the country.

This initial wave of immigrants, known as the First Aliyah (1881–1903), set the tone for the change that was to take place in the ancient land by introducing dozens of new crops like tea, cotton and tobacco as well as factories, clinics and schools.

They also substantially reinforced the traditional Jewish communities in Jaffa and Jerusalem. By the end of 1903 the Jews had purchased about 100,000

acres and had founded 23 new settlements.

The residents of Rosh Pina suffered their ups and downs, fighting off disease, attacks from neighbours and failed crops. But all that is behind them now. Rosh Pina today is a charming village and its old stone houses and cobbled lanes make it a much sought–after retreat.

Flying over the western part of Upper Galilee we can pick out the kibbutzim (collective farms) and Arab and Druse villages of this still mainly agricultural area. Each seems to live in an isolated world of its own. Groves of knarled olive trees, wheat fields and vineyards create a gentler landscape and we can almost smell the delicious aroma of pita bread being baked on round wood burning *taboun* stoves in the more traditional houses.

The recipes in Israel's kitchens come from every corner of the globe but a love of the Israeli–Palestinian versions of traditional Mediterranean food cuts across ethnic lines.
A roadside Galilee restaurant is the perfect setting for a traditional meal of pita, creamy *labaneh* goat's cheese flavoured with olive oil and *hyssop (za'atar)*, *houmous* (a paste of crushed chick peas) and *tehina* dip made from sesame seeds.

As our appetite grows we could add a main course of *siniya* (lamb roasted in tehina sauce) accompanied by small plates of pickles, olives, stuffed vine leaves and other salads all washed down with anis–based *arak*. For dessert, let's try a sweet *baclawa* pastry stuffed with honey and pistachio nuts while we sip from tiny cups of bitter black coffee poured from a curved coffee pot.

This part of the Galilee is attempting to blend these traditional delights with the needs of the 21st century. In the Tefen and Segev regions, clean hi–tech industrial parks are springing up near Arab villages, some of which still cling to the old ways.

The population of the Galilee is about half Arab and Druse and half Jewish. Of Israel's population of almost six million, nearly a million are Arab and seventy percent of these are Muslims. Israel also contains 100,000 Druse citizens, distinguished by the proud bearing and white turbans of their moustachioed elders, the guardians of their ancient faith.

Jethro, the father–in–law of Moses, is a central figure in Druse belief. He is "The Hidden Prophet" in-spiring the prophet of each generation. Soon after passing over the magnificent, isolated Crusader castle at Montfort that once housed the headquarters of the Teutonic Knights, we receive our first glimpse of the blue Mediterranean.

At the point where Israel's northern coast meets the southern coast of Lebanon, the shoreline is wild and rocky. Beneath the white cliffs at Rosh Hanikra the insistent pummeling of the waves has carved out grottoes reached by cable car. Nearby is the ancient site of Achziv, now surrounded by rolling lawns, one of more than 40 national parks dotted around the country containing important archaeological sites in protected park settings.

Continuing south down the coastline we come to an important historical crossroads—the port city of Acre (Acco). The history of Acre can be traced back to the Phoenicians. It was conquered by Alexander the Great in the 4th century BC and was the gateway for the Roman conquests. In the 12th century Acre became the capital of the Crusader kingdom.

The Crusaders might be surprised to discover that the subterranean vaults they built are now used as performance areas at the annual theater festival. Centuries after the Crusades, Napoleon met failure at Acre, falling back against the stiff resistance of the Ottoman "Butcher of Acre" Ahmad Jazzar Pasha. It was he who built Acre's magnificent ramparts and the great Al Jazr mosque.

The colonnades of the Khan el Umdan (Inn of the Columns) were erected in 1906 by the Ottoman Sultan Abdul Hamid. In Acre, these layers of civilization were built on top of one another, sometimes employing the building stones of the previous layer. As a result, Acre's Old City is now a magnificent cacophony of Gothic arches, Turkish minarets and Arab domes.

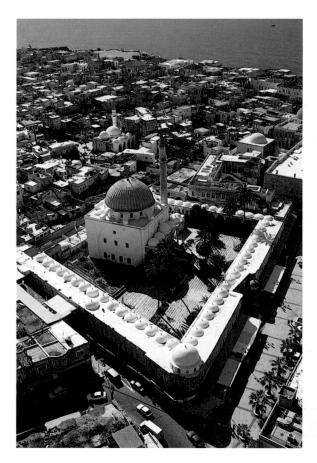

Turning back inland along the Beit Hakerem Valley, which divides the Upper Galilee from the Lower, we sweep over fields, olive groves and Arab towns to encounter the present at the new Israeli town of Carmiel.

A planned town, Carmiel has successfully absorbed thousands of new immigrants from the former Soviet Union. With its broad streets, modern neighborhoods and hi–tech plants it seems a world away from the chaotic jumble of Acre.

21 bottom Acre's port is now a haven for tourists and fishermen. Behind it lies the Khan al-Umdan (Inn of the Columns) with its double colonnades and typical Turkish clock tower. This was once part of the Genoese quarter of the earlier Crusader city.

20-21 Providing one of the few natural harbors along the coast and commanding access to the center of the country, Acre, or Acco, was regarded as the key to the Holy Land.

21 top Acre's White Mosque, an important Muslim site, built in 1781 by Jazzar Pasha, is thought to lie on top of the Crusader Church of the Holy Cross. Its interior contains some magnificent examples of multicolored marble and stone work.

Israel is dotted with sites of great historical and religious significance for millions of Christians all over the world. Flying due east from modern Carmiel we now approach an important concentration of Christian sites along the northern shores of the Sea of Galilee (called "The Sea of Gennesareth" by the New Testament and *Kinneret* or "harp" in modern Hebrew). It is here that Jesus of Nazareth walked, spread the gospel healed and performed the miracles mentioned in the Bible. Little wonder that this area has become a magnet for the multitudes of Christian pilgrims drawn to the "Evangelical Triangle" of Capernaum, Tabgha and the Mount of Beatitudes.

Capernaum (Kefar Nahum) was an important lakeside town when Jesus began his first ministry and is the site of several of his miracles including the healing of St. Peter's mother–in–law. Even though he was brought up

22 left A sightseeing boat chugging across the placid waters of the Sea of Galilee follows much the same route as that taken by Jesus and his disciples.

22-23 This Franciscan church was built in the 1930s on the Mount of Beatitudes, thought to be the site of the Sermon on the Mount. Exuding tranquility, it affords pilgrims an unparalleled view of the lake and the surrounding hills.

22 bottom The Chapel of the Primacy at Tabgha on the shores of the Sea of Galilee. Built in the 1930s out of local black basalt, its small interior recalls the discussion between the resurrected Christ and his disciple, Peter.

in Nazareth, Jesus was so often in Capernaum that it is referred to by Matthew and Mark as his "home town." It remained a small fishing village until the fourth century when it became a major focus for the development of the Christian community. The Greek Orthodox Chapel with its bright red domes was built among the ruins of the seventh century village. Capernaum also boasts a Franciscan church and a remarkable late fourth century synagogue, thought to have been built over an earlier synagogue from the time of Jesus.

Above Capernaum is the Mountain of the Beatitudes where, according to most Christian traditions, Jesus gave The Sermon On The Mount. In 1936, the domed octagonal church and a hospice were built on the spot, both run by Franciscan nuns. The church was designed by the famous Italian architect Antonio Barluzzi, who had a profound influence on modern church art and architecture in the Holy Land. This serene site also offers a magnificent view of the lake. Tabgha *(Heptapagon* or "the place of the seven springs" in Greek) is

thought to be the site of the Miracle of the Loaves and the Fishes and also of the appearance of Jesus to his disciples after his death, when the primacy of Peter was established. The original Byzantine Church of the Miracle of the Loaves and Fishes was built in the fifth century. Today's structure has incorporated its magnificent mosaics, one of which portrays a basket of bread flanked by two fish.

At Kibbutz Ginnosar, just north of Magdala, the home town of Mary Magdalene, a boat from time of Jesus was retrieved from the lake and is now being preserved. From the kibbutz wharf, groups of pilgrims embark on replicas of that ancient vessel to cross the normally placid waters of the lake. On the opposite shore, at one of the lakeside restaurants, they will enjoy one of the "St Peter's Fish" that abound in these waters. The Sea of Galilee is the lowest lake in the world (600 feet below sea level). It is also Israel's largest freshwater lake, the source of much of its potable water and subject of many of its songs.

The lakeside city of Tiberias, famous for centuries for its health–giving hot mineral springs, is now a popular winter resort where visitors from colder climes can thaw out in the water or in the rays of its sub–tropical climate. In fact, the banks of the Sea of Galilee are a popular holiday venue for ordinary Israelis who camp out, on the water's edge, often preparing meat over charcoal grills or a finely chopped salad of tomatoes, cucumbers and peppers.

This area also has special significance in the Muslim history of the Land of Israel. At the nearby Horns of Hittin, two summits flanking the crater of an extinct volcano, the Crusader army was defeated by Salah–a–Din (Saladin) in 1187, a defeat thath began the demise of the First Crusader Latin Kingdom of Jerusalem and led to Salah–a–Din's conquest of that city in the same year. Before leaving the Sea of Galilee let us stop off at another crucial landmark in the development of modern Israel or the *Yishuv* (Jewish community) that preceded it. At Rosh Pina we mentioned the First Aliyah, which established the *moshavot*. At the point where the Jordan runs out of the Sea of Galilee and continues on its meandering course, we find a symbol of the Second Aliyah (1904–1914), the "Mother of Kibbutzim" at the kibbutz of Degania Aleph.

Many of the pioneers of the Second Aliyah sought to create an ideal society that would integrate the ideas of national rebirth and social revolution based on Zionist–Socialist principles.

In 1909 a commune *(kevutza)* of Jewish workers made their home here. The *kevutza*, which later became the *kibbutz*, is by definition a settlement on state property, based on the labor of its members who live collectively. Among the leaders of the collective that settled at Degania was A. D. Gordon, one of the leading philosophers of the labour settlement movement that laid the foundations for the future state of Israel. Gordon developed the concept of the importance of physical labour into a doctrine that inspired generations of idealistic young Jewish pioneers.

Such ideas have little significance for most of today's young Israelis who are more likely to be influenced by the Internet and cable TV than by the utopian ideals of their pioneering forbears.

25 top Hidden behind the foliage of Kibbutz Degania, the Sea of Galilee pours into the River Jordan. At Yardenit, in a loop in the river, pilgrims undergo ritual baptism.

25 bottom The verdant fields of Kibbutz Ginnosar grow a variety of fruits, including bananas. Magdala, the home town of Mary Magdalene, lies just to the south.

24-25 Kibbutz Ginnosar on the western shore of the Sea of Galilee. The round structure on the water's edge houses a museum dedicated to the Galilee. The "Jesus Boat," an authentic boat from the time of Jesus, is undergoing preservation here.

26 top *The Crusader remains at Antipatris in the Afek national park east of Tel Aviv lie close to the sources of the Yarkon River and command a strategic section of the ancient Via Maris.*

26 bottom In the 12th century Migdal Tzedek or Migdal Afek, east of the modern city of Petah Tikva, was the site of a Crusader fortress called Mirabelle. Today's ruins are of the more recent Arab settlement of Majdal Yaba.

Our next stop, a few miles to the west, is another major Christian landmark—Nazareth. At the time of Joseph and Mary this was a hamlet with a population of no more than 400. Today it is the largest Arab city in Israel, a bustling town with a traffic problem.

In Nazareth the Virgin Mary received the Annunciation from the Angel Gabriel and Jesus later received his education and grew to manhood. Nazareth retained its Jewish character until the end of the Byzantine period but by the end of the sixth century it contained a full–fledged Christian community. The town was destroyed by the Mamelukes in the thirteenth century and

26-27 The church and monastery at Sepphoris (Zippori). In the Hasmonean and Herodian periods, Sepphoris was the capital of the Galilee. The first codification of Jewish oral law—the Mishna—was completed here by Juda Ha-Nasi who headed the Sanhedrin or high court established here after the destruction of the Temple in Jerusalem by the Romans.

only regained its status when its Christian institutions developed in the nineteenth century.

Nazareth is dotted with churches marking crucial events in the Gospels. The Basilica of the Annunciation is several churches in one. The present church with its distinctive spire was built in 1968 over the remains of two earlier Byzantine and Crusader churches, both of them resting on an ancient house that according to some traditions is the site of the Annunciation. The Orthodox tradition however places the site at the "Virgin's Fountain" near the Greek Orthodox Church of St. Gabriel. The Synagogue Church is built over the synagogue where Jesus is thought to have prayed and the Church of Mensa Christi (The Table of the Messiah) on the outskirts of Nazareth is considered to be the site where Jesus dined with his disciples after the Resurrection.

In its Declaration of Independence, Israel is described as a Jewish State, but anyone under the impression that it is just a Jewish state should consider the case of Nazareth. One of the most important Christian sites in the world, with a large Arab Christian population, the

majority of Nazareth's inhabitants are nevertheless Muslim. One in six Israelis is a Palestinian Arab. The Arab community mainly lives in the Galilee and in the central "Triangle" area. Jews and Arabs tend to live in separate communities but in towns like Tel Aviv–Jaffa, Haifa, Acre and Ramle, they live side by side.

Whatever the ethnic origin of Israel's inhabitants and be they Jewish, Muslim, Christian or Druse, it is the land where their histories unfolded that has tied them to this place. Zippori (Sepphoris) is such a place, illustrating a history that spans civilizations and religions. It lies not far from Nazareth on a hill surrounded by a fertile valley. "Zippori is sixteen miles around and most assuredly a land flowing with milk and honey" says the Jerusalem Talmud. From the air it is easy to imagine that Zippori's grid of ruined walls once contained a flourishing city.

The first settlement of Zippori probably began in the eighth century B.C. In 55 B.C. it was declared capital of Galilee under Roman domination. In the course of its history Zippori was razed to the ground, destroyed by an earthquake, rebuilt, flourished and waned. Herod captured it at the height of a snowstorm.

In the beginning of the third century it became the seat of the Sanhedrin, the highest judicial and ecclesiastical council of the Jewish nation. According to local tradition, Anne and Joachim, the parents of the Virgin Mary, had their home in Zippori and in the fourth century the first Byzantine church was built here. Under the Crusaders the town was called Le Saphorie and under the Arabs it became the village of Saffuriyyeh which existed until 1948. In 1949 a moshav (cooperative farm) established here took the ancient Hebrew name of Zippori.

Today the Zippori National Park allows the visitor to take a walk through these layers of civilization. Among its artistic treasures are magnificent mosaic floors from the Roman and Byzantine periods. The "Mona Lisa of the Galilee" depicts a woman of rare beauty while the fascinating "Nile Mosaic" depicts Egyptian festivals celebrating the high water peak of the Nile alongside hunting scenes.

It seems that whatever path we take in Israel, we are taking the path of history. Consider this list of invasion, conquest and settlement: Canaanites, Phoenicians, Hyksos, Israelites, Assyrians, Babylonians, Greeks, Ptolemies, Seleucids, Jewish Hasmoneans, Romans, Byzantines, Persians, Umayyad Muslims, Abbasids, Seljuks, Arabs, Mameluke Muslims, Egyptians, Turks, British, Israelis. The endless invasions of this vulnerable, strategic pathway, this Promised Land, have left behind some magnificent physical, intellectual and spiritual treasures but also a trail of bloodshed and woe. As if to illustrate how the long march of history, from ancient to modern times, has left its mark on one city we follow the wide course of the Jordan Valley, and come to Beit Shean. This ancient city

site, situated at an important crossroads, has a history spanning 4,000 years. The Philistines who ruled here displayed the bodies of King Saul and his sons on its walls after they had been killed in the Battle of Mount Gilboa. Beit Shean was conquered by King David and strengthened under King Solomon. In the Hellenistic period it was known as Scythopolis. In the Roman period it was also named Nysa, after the nurse of Dionysos, the god of wine, who according to tradition is buried here. The Jews of the Land of Israel later called Beit Shean "The Gateway to the Garden of Eden" because of its rich gardens fed by springs. The city reached its peak during the 6th century after Christ when its population burgeoned to more than 30,000 but was destroyed suddenly

in the great earthquake of 749. Today's visitor to the Beit Shean National Park can clearly appreciate the scope of the city with its magnificent theater, temple, amphitheater, streets and public buildings.

In contrast, the modern town of Beit Shean is rather nondescript. It is one of the many "development towns" hurriedly established in outlying areas in the 1950s and 60s for the hundreds of thousands of new Jewish immigrants to Israel, mainly from the North African and Arab states. Mainly situated in outlying areas like the Galilee and the Negev, these development towns were a social experiment born out of urgent necessity to disperse a growing population but, with a few exceptions, they have always lagged behind the larger urban centers. The disaffection of these immigrants, known as *Sephardim* or *Mizrachim*, remains a major social and political issue. Israel's history and population mix has created a confusion of religions, cultures, traditions and ethnic identities. And not only do Jews, Christians and Muslims have to co–exist. Finding common ground between Jews originating from Fez and Vienna, Georgia and Algiers, Baghdad and New York City is no simple matter either.

28-29 The theater at Beit Shean, or Scythopolis as it was called by the Romans, lay at the end of one of the city's main colonnaded streets and held up to 5,000 spectators.

29 Beit Shean has been inhabited for some 6,000 years. In the Hellenistic period the city moved to the foot of the flat–topped hill and in the Roman period Scythopolis, with its magnificent temples and public buildings, became one of ten city–states known as the Decapolis.

Modern Israel's founding fathers with their European socialist backgrounds, adopted the idea of a Jewish melting pot out of which they hoped would emerge "an Israeli." But cultures moulded over centuries cannot be melted away that easily. The traditions and family structures of the Sephardim were insensitively disregarded in the rush to build a new nation, leading to alienation and protest that has been passed on to the second and third generations of the original Sephardi immigrants. At the same time, the melting pot has to an extent worked by means of intermarriage between Sephardi and Ashkenazi (European) Jews. Also, in recent years, there has been a change in attitude and the cultures and traditions of Israel's various communities are again being preserved and celebrated with pride. Sometimes, the various strands of eastern and western cultures intertwine in works of art and ways of living that are a unique synthesis of their disparate elements. These are perhaps more "Israeli" than forced attempts to fit people into a mold.

If the development town of Beit Shean represents

Israel's quest for a multicultural society, the rich, fertile Jezreel Valley to the north–east takes us back to the pioneering days of the Second Aliyah and its revolutionary and utopian ideas of socialism, Jewish labor cooperative living and social equality. The Second Aliyah contained more than its fair share of dreamers, radicals and poets and not all were able to adapt to the tough labor and harsh conditions of the period.

The spartan credo of the kibbutz—"Every member gives according to his ability and receives according to his needs" was typical of their radical thinking and proved not always possible to implement, but it was an efficient means of pooling precious resources and contending with numerous difficulties. This was a major transformation for a people who in the diaspora had for centuries been bound not only by their own religious edicts and hierarchical family structures but also by the limited number of occupations imposed upon them.

In ancient times the Jezreel Valley was part of the ancient Via Maris road followed by invading armies, merchants and travelers making their way from Egypt, through the Land of Israel to Syria and Lebanon. But by the time the lands of the valley were purchased in 1921 they mostly amounted to swamp. By 1930 the valley had been drained and more than twenty new settlements had been established here. Among them

were the first kibbutz in the valley at Ein Harod.

The first *moshav*—a cooperative farm less stringently collective than a kibbutz—was founded here in 1921 at Nahalal. Collectives such as these played a formative role in the settlement and defense of the Jewish community (the *Yishuv*) before the State of Israel was created. They also created a unique society: democratic, secular, self–sufficient, cooperative, connected to the land and to nature. Ironically, despite the crucial role played by Israel's kibbutz movements, the kibbutz population has never exceeded a few percent of the total. In today's free–market economy, kibbutzim are undergoing something of an identity crisis and are seeking ways to integrate within a fast changing economic and social environment.

30-31 Nahalal in the Jezreel
Valley, the first moshav in what
was then Palestine, was founded
in 1921 by pioneers from
Degania dissatisfied with the
restrictive social patterns of the
kibbutz. Unlike a kibbutz, moshav
members hold private property.

31 bottom The hub–and–spoke
layout of Nahalal, like that
of many early agricultural
settlements, was designed
for defensive purposes: homes
and communal buildings were
situated in the center followed
by outhouses and fields.

From the cradle of Israeli agriculture, we cross the Carmel mountain range to visit one of the cradles of Israel's industry, at the Mediterranean city of Haifa. A no–nonsense, hardworking town, Haifa is Israel's third largest city, a major port and the commercial and industrial and hi–tech capital of the north. It was here in 1920 that the Histadrut labour federation held its founding convention, declaring as its aims to unite and unionise all workers who earn their living without exploiting the work of others. In the years that followed, the Histadrut developed a plethora of enterprises, industries, schools, settlements, health services, cultural institutions and defense organizations that made it inseparable from the emerging state itself. Two of Israel's prime ministers—David Ben–Gurion and Golda Meir—first served in the post of Secretary—General of the His-

tadrut. Today, the Histadrut has lost most of its former power to privatization and resembles other labour organizations. Strangely, the most recognized landmark of Haifa, where the Histadrut was born, is the exotic Bahai center with its magnificent, manicured gardens. These cut a symmetrical green path up Mount Carmel culminating in the golden dome and Corinthian–style columns of the shrine.

Let's wing down the coastline now. It will be almost a straight run. Israel's coastline traces a long gentle curve and contains some magnificent white beaches but no natural ports. Divers excavating off small coastal communities like Atlit, Ma'agan Michael and Habonim, regularly unearth ancient bottles and vases from sunken vessels caught in a squall and unable to put in at port. King Herod (a cruel despot but a great builder) decided to

32-33 A Roman aqueduct, a modern fleet of vehicles and an eastern meditation group on the beach at Caesaria. Such juxtapositions of the secular and the sacred, the ancient and the modern, make Israel a country in which surprises are almost commonplace.

33 top The coastline at Kibbutz Ga'ash, north of Tel Aviv, is formed out of kurkar, a rock consisting of fused sand, which leaves only a narrow strip of beach.

33 bottom The national park at Achziv on the Mediterranean coast of the western Galilee forms a natural lagoon, a popular venue for families from the area.

34-35 The restored Roman theater at Caesaria is the perfect setting for an open-air concert on a balmy night. Formerly a Phoenician port, Caesaria was rebuilt by King Herod as a grand Hellenistic city, both in homage to his patron Caesar Augustus and as a monument to his own sovereignty and power.

solve the problem of the straight coastline by building, around 50 B.C., a huge artificial port at Caesaria much of which has been unearthed in recent years. The outlines of Caesaria, with its defensive walls, theater, amphitheater, public buildings, commercial and living quarters can be made out clearly from the air. In the middle of his city, Herod built a podium on which he placed a magnificent temple dedicated to Rome and to his patron Caesar Octavius Augustus. Sometimes a site assumes a mantle of sanctity that is transferred from one religion to another. Hence in the Byzantine period Herod's temple at Caesaria became a church, in the Arab Period it was transformed into a mosque while under the Crusaders a cathedral was built here. Today, most visitors to Caesaria are more likely to be seeking a rock concert at the restored theater than a place of worship.

As we swoop down the busy coastal highway, the landscape of citrus groves and sand dunes gives way to new industrial and commercial building. Theodore Herzl (1860–1904), the founder of modern political Zionism and the "visionary of the state" would have difficulty in recognizing Herzliya, the modern city named after him. For now we are approaching the heartland of modern Israel, the sprawling urban conurbation known as the Dan Bloc, which is home for one–third of the population. For better or for worse, the symbol of the pioneer–farmer has all but disappeared from the Israeli consciousness. And why indeed should it have remained, when 90 per cent of Israelis are city dwellers. Like urbanites everywhere, they are more concerned with cutting commuting time than bringing in the crops.

Tel Aviv–Jaffa is the core of the Dan Bloc. Founded in 1908, Tel Aviv, the first all–Jewish city in modern times, began as a garden suburb of Jaffa, its ancient neighbor. In the 20's it burgeoned from a total population of only 3,604 in 1921 to over 54,000 by 1931. In the early decades European immigrant architects and artists, influenced by the Arab buildings they saw around them, tried to give the new city an "eastern" feel. In the 30's and 40's a new influx of architects, some leading proponents of the German Bauhaus school, turned Tel

Aviv into a "White City" of sleek apartment buildings designed in the International Style. In recent years the low skyline has been transformed by tall office buildings, one of the signs of Israel's rapid development. Tel Aviv is Israel's cosmopolitan business, commercial, cultural and entertainment capital. Like every Israeli city, it is a mirror of the various cultures that make up its population. To connect with the east, wander around the Carmel open air market or a district like Florentine with its maze of little shops selling everything from flaky *bourekas* pastries to pots and pans. To connect with western here and now, watch the Friday afternoon parade of the young trendy

set on Sheinkin Street from a pavement cafe or check out the latest fashions at the Dizengoff Center shopping mall. Tel Aviv is Israel's good–time town, packed with cafes, restaurants, cinemas, bars and clubs that cater toevery taste. On weekends the city is still buzzing at 3 a.m.: little wonder that Tel Aviv has earned the title "the city that never stops." Many of Tel Aviv's cultural institutions, like the Israel Philharmonic and the Habima National Theater, were founded well before the State of Israel came into being. These laid the foundation for a lively cultural scene that provides for tastes as disparate as Opera and belly dancing, Shakespeare and stand–up.

36 left Tel Aviv's marina and its beach front string of sleek hotels exemplify Israel's new prosperity.

36 bottom The characteristic low skyline of Tel Aviv is being transformed by new towers. To the surprise of visitors the city contains the largest concentration of Bauhaus architecture anywhere.

36-37 Tel Aviv's shoreline as seen from Jaffa in the south.

38-39 The large square was once called "Square of the Kings of Israel." The scene of numerous exhibitions, festivals and demonstrations, its name was changed to Rabin Square after Israeli Prime Minister Yitzhak Rabin was assassinated here in November 1995.

40-41 Archaeological excavations of the monumental buildings at the southeast corner of the Temple Mount. The flight of steps which seem to end nowhere once led to the Double Gate of the Second Temple, destroyed by the Romans in A.D. 70.

If Tel Aviv is Israel's avant–guard, Jaffa, out of which it grew, is one of the oldest cities in the world. According to one legend it was established before the Flood. Conquered by the Egyptians in the fifteenth century B.C., its port and strategic position turned it into an important maritime gateway to the Holy Land and a central point in the Via Maris between Egypt and the Fertile Crescent. In later times Jaffa also served as Jerusalem's port, which may explain why one of Jerusalem's gates, is called Jaffa Gate. It was through Jaffa that the Cedars of Lebanon were brought for the construction of Solomon's Temple in Jerusalem. In 1099 the Crusaders burst through Jaffa on their way to Jerusalem and under the period of Turkish rule it was the gateway to Jerusalem for Christian pilgrims. In Napoleon's sweep along Israel's coastal plane in 1799, Jaffa fell to the French army after a three–day seige. After failing to take Acre, Napoleon fell back to Jaffa before returning to Egypt and leaving Palestine to the Turks.

40 top Jaffa Gate, one of the main entrances to the Old City, marks the dividing line between the Armenian Quarter to the south and the Christian Quarter to the north.

40 bottom The Ophel, where King Solomon built magnificent royal buildings leading to his Temple.

Today, Jaffa's restored Old City is the habitat of artists and craftsmen, and a popular venue for tourists who can wander its alleyways. With its quaint restaurants, Jaffa is probably the most typically Mediterranean of Israel's towns.

In the land of contrasts that is Israel, the contrast between Tel Aviv and Jerusalem is perhaps the most striking. The short journey from Tel Aviv to Jerusalem takes us up from the coastal plane to the crest of the central mountain range, and from a thrusting, modern city to an ageless, solemn, city–site sacred to three religions. For Israelis, Tel Aviv symbolizes modernity, freedom and secular liberalism while Jerusalem symbolizes faith, piety and the constraints of an unchanging religion. It is these two forces that are tugging against each other in modern Israeli society and which many believe will set the national agenda in the years to come. Approaching Jerusalem one feels a numinous sense of ascending to a place imbued with spir-

ituality. Indeed, since the site has no particular strategic importance or natural advantages it was perhaps its light which first attracted the ancients to this area. At twilight the hilltops around the city are crowned in a radiant halo. As the last rays of the sun strike the domes of the Old City, the yellow stone buildings emit a final golden blush. In the strong sunlight of a summer's day, Jerusalem's light is so intense that visitors often feel that scales have been removed from their eyes.

Always shrouded in mysticism, this hill–city was founded in the third millennium B.C. King David, after shattering the power of the Philistines, captured the city from the Jebusites in the 10th century B.C. thereby completing the conquest of Canaan. David was the first to make Jerusalem a political and military capital but by moving the Ark of the Covenant to Jerusalem, he also made the city the eternal spiritual capital of the Jewish people. The Ark of the Covenant, thought to be inhabited

by the Supreme Being, had accompanied the Israelite tribes throughout their long wanderings and battles. Now David, "brought the ark of the Lord, and set it in his place, in the midst of the tabernacle that David had pitched for it." (II Samuel vi.) With the most sacred national and religious symbol of Israel now permanently situated in Jerusalem, the sanctity of the city to Jews was ensured.

King Solomon dedicated his magnificent First Temple here in 954 B.C. Its foundation stone was considered the center of the world, the place from where Creation had commenced. Jerusalem's cosmic significance also derives from the belief that it is the Divine footstool underneath God's throne and a mirror image of the "Heavenly Jerusalem" that one day will be united with the "Earthly Jerusalem." In another sense, Jerusalem symbolises the messianic hope for the "ingathering of the exiles" and the institution of the Divine Kingdom on earth.

In the squares of Jerusalem the prophets Isaiah and Jeremiah uttered words that have had a profound influence on moral and religious thinking. It was in the period of these prophets that the Temple in Jerusalem became the site of pilgrimage and sacrifice. Three times a year, on festivals still celebrated, the menfolk would make pilgrimage to Jerusalem at the Temple: on Passover (Pesach), marking the exodus of the Children of Israel from their bondage in Egypt; Tabernacles (Succot), recalling the temporary shelters they erected on their wanderings and on The Feast of Weeks (Shavuot), the celebration of the granting of the Torah to Moses on Mount Sinai.

In 587 B.C. the walls of Jerusalem were breached by the Babylonian emperor Nebuchadnezzar, who destroyed the Temple, laid the city to waste, and carried off the survivors to exile in Babylon. It was "by the waters of Babylon" that the longing for Jerusalem of the Psalmists was expressed that has echoed down through the generations:

"How shall we sing the Lord's song in a strange land?

If I forget thee, O Jerusalem, let my right hand forget her cunning.

If I do not remember thee, let my tongue cleave to the roof of my mouth;

If I prefer not Jerusalem over my chief joy."

The purification of the Temple by Judah the Maccabee after it had been defiled by the pagan Seleucid Greeks in the second century B.C., marked the beginning of the Jewish Hasmonean dynasty and the source of another Jewish holiday—Hanukkah.

According to legend, when the Hasmoneans came to dedicate the Temple sanctuary there was only enough pure oil in the sacramental jar for one day, yet ,through the blessing of God, it lasted for eight days until a fresh supply became available. Jerusalem was captured by the Roman general Pompey in 63 B.C. and it was under Roman patronage that Herod the Great was named king. Herod refurbished the Temple in magnificent style, probably to appease his subjects, who were deeply hostile to his allegiance to Rome. He also built a Royal Palace in Jerusalem and enlarged the foreboding Antonia fortress. But the Temple was his masterpiece. Great buttressed walls supported the massive platform housing

the gold–facaded Temple sanctuary with its outer and inner courts culminating in the Holy of Holies. The rabbinical sages may not have agreed with Herod's politics but they were moved by the splendor of his magnificent shrine.

After gazing with wonder at Herod's Temple they wrote that Jerusalem was, "blessed with nine measures of beauty." Following the destruction of Jerusalem and of the Temple by Titus in A.D. 70, sacrifices were replaced by liturgy but Jerusalem remained a religious focus and the supreme object of spiritual longing, and Jews everywhere have directed their prayers to Jerusalem ever since. The Western, or Wailing, Wall, is a remnant of the outer retaining wall of the Temple compound and is the holiest place in Judaism and one of its enduring symbols. In the cracks of the massive stones, people from all over the world place notes containing their deepest wishes. Devout Jews still throng to the

Western Wall at festival times and it is a popular site to hold "baremitzvah" (confirmation) ceremonies of 13–year–old boys who have reached the age of manhood under Jewish Law.

Parts of Herod's Temple were still under construction when Jesus of Galilee came to Jerusalem for what was to be his last Passover meal, later to become known as The Last Supper. This is traditionally believed to have taken place on what is today Mount Zion, just outside the existing walls of the Old City, built by the Ottoman ruler Sultan Suleiman the Magnificent in the 16th century.

The Last Supper is recalled in the Coenaculum chapel on Mount Zion. In fact the presumed location of every event in the final hours of the charismatic preacher, who upset both the Jewish establishment and the Roman occupiers by calling himself The Son of God, is now marked by a shrine or a church.

42 top The black–domed El-Aksa mosque although less impressive architecturally than the Dome of the Rock, is more important as a center of prayer and can accommodate up to 5,000 worshippers.

42 bottom Devout Jewish worshippers streaming to the Western, or Wailing, Wall. Ultra-orthodox men,

dressed in black, are separated from the smaller women's section.

42-43 Jerusalem at the time of King David covered the narrow spur south of the Temple Mount that is now the village of Silwan or Siloam. Many adherents of the three monotheistic religions consider Jerusalem to be the center of the world.

It was the Christian Emperor Constantine who canceled the name the Romans had given to Jerusalem—Aelia Capitolina—and who, with his mother, Queen Helena, rediscovered and restored the sites mentioned in the Gospels.

The first and most important of these was the Church of the Holy Sepulcher, built by Queen Helena in A.D. 325 to mark the site of the Crucifixion and Resurrection. This was built above a Temple to Venus erected by the Emperor Hadrian, that Helena had removed. With its central rotunda of the Anastasis (Resurrection of Christ) it was to

44-45 The Mount of Olives is dotted with churches and shrines abutting the ancient Jewish cemetery. The Church of All Nations (Church of the Agony) by the roadside was built by the Franciscans in 1924. Above it, at Gethsemane, is the Russian Orthodox Church of Mary Magdalene with its seven onion-shaped domes.

become the goal of all Christian pilgrimages and the most sacred of Christian holy places. Its destruction by the Caliph Hakim in 1010 was one of the central reasons for the Crusades. Six Christian communities—Greek Orthodox, Armenian, Roman Catholic, Syrian Orthodox, Coptic and Ethiopian—now hold daily prayers here.

Winding its way through the arches and alleyways of the Old City is the Via Dolorosa, "The Way of Sorrow" Jesus followed on the fateful journey from His condemnation by Pontias Pilate to the Crucifixion. The route takes pilgrims from the remains of the Roman Antonia fortress to the Church of the Holy Sepulcher via fourteen stations of prayer. Each Friday the Franciscan Order takes pilgrims along these Stations of the Cross in a tradition dating from the fourteenth century. Chapels and shrines– The Chapel of the Flagellation, The Chapel of the Condemnation, the Ecce Homo chapel and others—mark the path.

Many of Jerusalem's churches are built on the slopes of the Mount of Olives, which is also the site of an ancient Jewish cemetery. Near the Garden of Gethsemane with its knarled olive trees lies The Church of the Agony whose dramatic artwork recalls the betrayal by Judas. Also nearby are the subterranean Tomb of the Virgin Mary and the Church of St. Mary Magdalene with its seven splendid onion–shaped spires commissioned by Czar Alexander III and maintained by White Russian nuns.

In 638 the Muslim armies under the Caliph Omar reached Byzantine Jerusalem and took it without bloodshed. So began the Muslim rule over Jerusalem and the veneration of the city by the third great monotheistic religion. In early Muslim tradition Mohammed had a vision in which he was carried on his legendary steed el–Burak from Mecca to the Jewish Temple in Jerusalem. From there he made his mystic flight through the seven heavens into the presence of the Almighty. It

45 The cupolas of the Church of All Nations mirror the domes of the Old City across the Kidron Valley.

was therefore on the Temple compound, renamed "Haram esh–Sharif" ("The Noble Sanctuary") that Omar built a wooden mosque that was transformed by 691 into the magnificent golden–domed structure known as the Mosque of Omar. It is also known as the Dome of the Rock because it is built over a rock from which Muslims believe Mohammed made his flight to the heavens. It is also the site of Mount Moriah where Abraham was commanded to sacrifice his son Isaac and the site of the Holy of Holies in the Jewish Temple. Each of the eight outer walls of this superb structure is graced with slender arches and the building is approached on all sides by broad flights of steps. The giant cupola is supported by an inner circle of pillars and directly beneath it lies the Rock—as–Sakhra in Arabic. The ceiling, richly decorated in gold and mosaics, is encircled by sixteen stained glass windows bordered by mosaics containing inscriptions from the Koran.

Nearby, still on the Temple Mount, is the silver domed El Aksa Mosque. Originally built in the eighth century, it was restored by Saladin, who added the beautiful *mihrab* or niche for the imam who leads prayers. But there are few more magnificent sites than the

Dome of the Rock seen from the Mount of Olives at dawn. The first rays of the sun illuminate the golden dome with a light that seems to fill not only Jerusalem but the whole world.

Most of the important sites we have mentioned, and many we have not, can be found within the labyrinth inside the Old City of Jerusalem, the area surrounded by Suleiman the Magnificent's sixteenth century walls and punctuated by its seven gates. This is divided into quarters—Muslim, Jewish, Christian and Armenian—each with its own distinctive character. The colorful bazaars are a magnet for tourists who throng shops packed with carpets and leather goods, jewelery, vegetables and spices, *darbuka* drums and olivewood souvenirs.

It is not unusual to encounter the devout representatives of Jerusalem's three religions hurrying along the vaulted alleyways: a Christian priest in flowing black robes, bearing the sign of the Cross; a Palestinian Arab in a gallabiyeh robe and traditional keffiye headdress; a black–clad Hassidic Jew with furlined hat and sidecurls. Each lives according to the prescriptions of his own faith and each also harkens to the sounds of his own religion: the pealing of church bells; the muezzin calling the Muslim faithful to prayer; the blowing of the *shofar* or ram's horn on the High Holy Days of the Jewish calen-

dar. The Old City contains the majority of Jerusalem's sacred monuments but covers only a fraction of what is Israel's largest city. The New City which began to spread out beyond the Old City in the latter half of the nineteenth century, is the capital and the seat of national institutions. Israel's parliament (the Knesset), the Hebrew University, the Supreme Court, the Israel Museum and the Yad Vashem Holocaust Memorial are the modern symbols of Israel's statehood. The New City is also a mosaic of peoples and cultures. In the ultra–orthodox Jewish neighborhoods such as Mea Shearim the daily life of its zealously religious inhabitants resembles that of traditional eastern European townships. Neighbourhoods like Nahlaot and Mahane Yehuda can sometimes conjure up the sounds and aromas of Morocco or Tunisia. East Jerusalem has an Arab majority and is an important commercial and cultural center for Palestinians.

46 The Lion's Gate provides entry to the Muslim Quarter from the east. To its north, outside the walls, lies the Muslim cemetery.

47 Damascus Gate, the main gateway to the Muslim Quarter, is built over an earlier gate built by

Hadrian for Roman Jerusalem—Aelia Capitolina. The Old City of Jerusalem still follows Hadrian's division of the city into four quarters. The main street follows the Cardo Maximus, which divides the city from north to south.

48 top The Mar Saba monastery perches precariously on top of a gorge in the Kidron Valley south of Jerusalem. Monks desiring even greater isolation could find it in niches cut out of the rock.

48 bottom Bethlehem, the birthplace of Jesus Christ, draws hundreds of thousands every year to celebrate the Nativity. The Church of the Nativity, built in the shape of a cross, was first erected by the Byzantine Queen Helena in 329.

Jerusalem has a million stories to tell, but it is time to move on to another city that is etched in the global consciousness—Bethlehem.

Situated a few miles south of Jerusalem, on the edge of the desert, Bethlehem is mentioned in several Bible stories. It was the birthplace of King David and centuries later of the Christian Messiah, Jesus Christ. "But you Bethlehem, Ephrata, out of you shall He come forth," foretold the prophet Micah. The Church of the Nativity, the most popular of Bethlehem's churches, is built above the cave thought to have been the manger of Jesus" Nativity. Queen Helena dedicated the first Church of the Nativity here in A.D. 329 and today it is shared by churches of all denominations. The cave inside it includes two small lobes, one with a star to mark the place of Jesus" birth, the other to mark the repose

of the Holy Family. Bethlehem, most of whose inhabitants are Christians, is controlled today by the Palestinian Authority, which now arranges the annual Christmas celebrations.

From the ethereal heights of Jerusalem and Bethlehem we are heading for the depths of the Dead Sea. Our flight path takes us through the rounded hills of the Judean Desert, a place of refuge for mystics, monks and kings. The semi–arid Judean Desert contains perhaps the most "biblical" landscape in Israel. In the folds and clefts of the bare hillsides it is common to come across an encampment of Bedouin whose way of life has hardly changed for centuries. Flocks of sheep and goats change the patterns across the rock and scrub. The quiet and solitude of this region also make it a perfect spot for uninterrupted contemplation. Sixteen hundred years ago early Christian communities built isolated monasteries here, like the Mar Saba monastery perched precariously above the water-cut canyon of the Kidron Valley, an almost surrealistic site when viewed from above. The seemingly inhospitable desert bursts into life after the winter rains when the

hillsides are covered with a carpet of grass and wild flowers. The vitality of springtime in the desert is what inspired the unknown author of the Song of Songs to write, "Rise up my love, my fair one, and come away./ For, lo, the winter is past./ The rain is over and gone:/ The flowers appear on the earth:/ The time of the singing of birds has come,/ And the voice of the turtle–dove is heard in our land..."

Before reaching the lowest sea on earth let us make a short detour to the lowest city on earth and the oldest fortified city on earth—Jericho, also part of the Palestinian Authority. Fed by natural springs, Jericho is an oasis, a splash of green, standing out against the desert background. Its rich fields, groves and orchards make it a popular spot to buy dates, citrus fruits and vegetables. The walls that Joshua sent "tumbling down" have yet to be found at the archaeological excavations at the site of ancient Jericho. Nevertheless, the remains of twenty–three city civilizations built and destroyed on this site, the earliest about 7,000 years old, bears out the fact that Jericho was the strategic eastern gateway to the Land of Israel.

48-49 Metsukei Dragot in the Judean Desert is a center for desert sports. Depending on how much space they want to cover, the adventurous can choose to explore the desert by jeep or by camel.

50-51 The new town of Ma'ale Adumim spreads over a Judean desert hilltop like the fingers of mankind encroaching into the pristine wilderness.

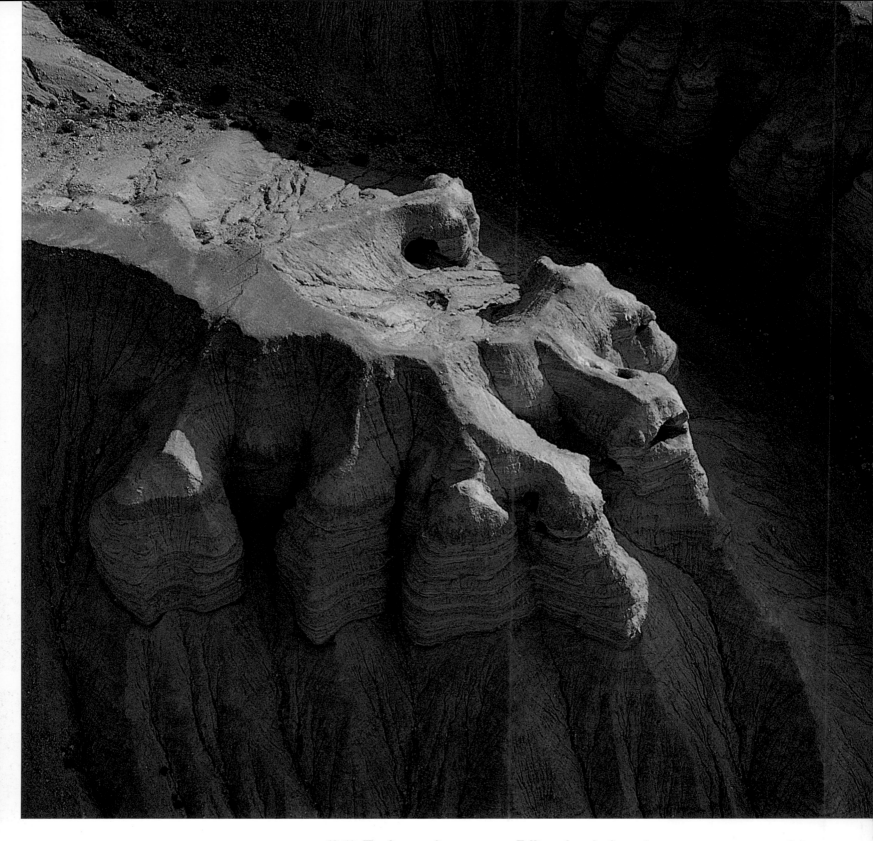

52-53 *The Qumran Caves where the Dead Sea Scrolls were discovered in 1947. Some researchers have attributed these writings and the remains of a nearby community to the Essenes, a Jewish sect.*

Falling sharply from the eastern escarpment of the Judean Desert and due south of Jericho lies the Dead Sea. Thirteen hundred feet below sea level, it is the lowest place on earth and the final outlet of the River Jordan. Devoid of life, it is a rich source of potash, magnesium, bromine and other minerals. The Dead Sea's waters, which have the highest level of salinity anywhere, make it impossible to drown. The buoyancy has to be experienced to be believed, the most common test being to sit up in the water and read a newspaper. This area has an almost lunar landscape made more unreal by the sharp contrast of the desert meeting the sea. It has nevertheless developed a tourist industry based on year-round sunshine, mineral spas and the Dead Sea mud that visitors smear over their bodies.

Even these inhospitable shores have been inhabited throughout the ages. Ein Gedi is mentioned in the Bible, its natural springs supporting tropical crops like dates and the

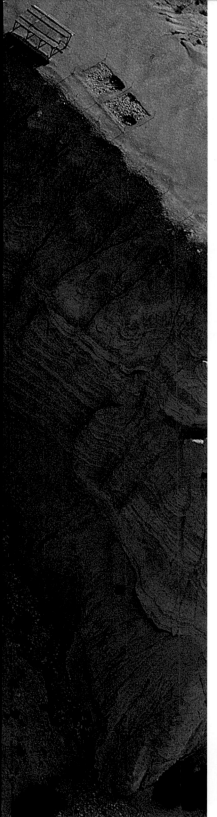

53 top Near ancient Qumran, the modern kibbutz of Kalya demonstrates that, with some ingenuity, life can be supported even on the desolate western shores of the Dead Sea.

53 bottom Built on a flat mountain top, Masada is separated from the surrounding desert plateau by steep slopes, making it the perfect desert refuge. The hanging or Northern Palace was an architectural feat used mainly by Herod for entertaining.

persimmon bush that yielded a valuable perfume. Today it is the site of a kibbutz and an archaeological park, and is a popular venue for hikers who can escape the blinding heat of the desert by wandering around its rich foliage and cool waterfalls. There are few joys on earth to match the exhilaration of showering under a natural waterfall after a long desert hike. Rock rabbits and gazelles are among the animals that inhabit this area and the very fortunate might even catch sight of one of the leopards who are protected in this nature reserve.

Two sites along the Dead Sea have been etched into Israel's consciousness. The first is Qumran, the site of a break–away Jewish sect known as the Essenes who lived here between the end of the 2nd century B.C. and the Great Revolt of the Jews against the Romans in the first century after Christ. They left behind them the magnificent legacy of writings known as the Dead Sea Scrolls, the first of which

were discovered by Bedouin shepherds in 1947. Some of these are kept in the Shrine of the Book in Jerusalem.

The second is Masada. At the summit of an isolated mountain and surrounded on all sides by gorges, Masada was chosen by Herod the Great as a place of retreat from his enemies. Here he built fortifications and palaces for himself and his court.

The Roman–Jewish historian Josephus Flavius described this desert fortress as "... fortified by Heaven and man alike against any enemy who might wage war against it." At the outset of the Great Revolt against the Romans in A.D. 66, a group of Jewish Zealots conquered Masada and later held out for months against the thousands of Roman soldiers who laid siege to the fortress. Eventually, when all hope was lost they decided to take their own lives rather than be captured. This proud and desperate act has turned Masada into a symbol of national determination.

Leaving Masada and the Dead Sea behind us we now begin our southward flight over the Negev desert. Covering about half of Israel's land mass but containing less than ten per cent of its population, the Negev is still only sparsely populated.

David Ben–Gurion, Israel's founding father and its first prime minister, believed that the greening and the settlement of the wide expanses of the Negev would be the next great Zionist enterprise.

In his later years he made a personal commitment to that vision by moving to the Negev kibbutz of Sdeh Boker where he is buried. Far from the pollution of the big cities, the Negev air is clean, hot and dry in the daytime and cool at night when the stars put on a spectacular stellar show.

54 top Tel Sheva, the mound of biblical Beersheba, is a few miles east of the modern city and symbolised the southern boundary of the Land of Israel. In the eighth century B.C., Beersheba was the provincial capital of the southern part of the Kingdom of Judah.

The Negev has been an inhabited desert for centuries and is criss–crossed with trails. The most famous of these is the Spice Route, controlled by the Nabateans, and linked by a network of trading posts and towns. The Nabateans established these settlements as far back as the fourth century B.C. They began as merchants, transporting herbs and spices from Arabia across the Negev to the port of Gaza, even exporting Dead Sea asphalt to the Egyptians, who used it for embalming. By the Byzantine period, the Nabateans were not only speaking Greek but also had become expert farmers and their cities had grown and flourished.

Modern–day Israel, a pioneer in the use of drip irrigation, is trying, with considerable success, to emulate the agricultural achievements of the ancient

Nabatean farmers. The result is that the barren Negev and the Arava Valley are the source of much of the exotic fruits and flowers that end up in European markets.

The city of Beersheba is the Negev's capital and Israel's fourth largest city. Although situated in the milder climactic zone of the northern desert, temperatures here are quire warm in August.

Once a week, a colorful Bedouin market is held here. Camels and goats, saddles and hand–woven carpets are bought and sold alongside more prosaic goods. Beersheba is another of the cities that in recent years has absorbed thousands of new immigrants from the former Soviet Union.

The incongruous sight of Russian speakers trading with Bedouin merchants is one example of Israel's disarming cultural kaleidoscope.

54 bottom The Negev Monument, designed by Israeli artist Dani Karavan, is a tribute to the Israeli forces that captured Beersheba from the Egyptian army in the War of Independence. Karavan was among them.

54-55 Beersheba, the capital of the Negev, is now Israel's fourth largest city and boasts a popular university.

56-57 The dry wadi (river bed) of Nahal Faran slices through the desert rock.

The northern Negev has enough rainfall to support seasonal cereal crops and pasture land and there is a large concentration of Bedouin tribes here. Constrained by controls on the use of land and by economic forces, the traditional Bedouin nomadic cycles have largely given way to farming and urban occupations. Yet many still live simple lives under the shade of their goatskin canvases and will extend to you the hospitality to strangers for which they are famous. Whether loping across the desert on a camel, or walking for miles along paths known only to them, the Bedouin and the desert are one.

Further south, the terrain becomes more rugged and the climate hotter and more arid. But for some, the desert is a playground. A variety of sports activities have developed around natural features like the three craters—the Ramon Crater, the Large Crater and the Small Crater. These can be crossed by jeep or camel, scaled by teams of rock climbers or, for the very daring, windsurfed over. Israel's standard of living has risen to European levels, transforming many of the country's formerly modest hikers into fully equipped sensation-seekers. The Ramon Crater is the biggest crater on earth and the largest nature reserve in Israel. twenty-five miles long, 6 miles wide and cutting 1,200 feet deep, this massive scoop out of the earth's crust displays a broad range of colors and geological strata.

The southern Negev has an annual rainfall of about one inch, but when the rains come, they can be torrential. With the rocky ground unable to absorb so

58-59 Founded by the Nabateans in the fourth century B.C., Avdat was a way station along the famous Spice Route along which perfumes, herbs, spices and other treasures were transported from the Orient to the Mediterranean.

much water, rivulets form into flash floods racing down the wadis carrying everything in their path. For people living in such conditions, the key to survival is to conserve water.

The Nabatean city dwellers of Avdat and Mamshit, both of which have been partly restored, created intricate systems of dams and cisterns to trap as much flood water as they could and succeeded in supporting flourishing and affluent communities. Today, water, still a precious commodity, is pumped in from the north.

59 top The visitor center at Mitzpe Ramon, overlooking the Ramon Crater, created by wind erosion.

59 bottom Mount Nishpeh. The hard rock at the summit withstands natural erosion while the softer material beneath it is worn away.

Now in the final stretch of our trans–Israel flight, we race down the Arava Valley in the eastern Negev. In fact we are reconnecting with the Syrian–African Rift as it plunges into the Red Sea. Almost blinded by the sun reflected off the bright chalk and limestone valley bed we are surprised by sudden patches of green below as we fly over agricultural communities.

Near the kibbutz of Yodfata, for example, a nature reserve has been set aside to reintroduce animal species that once roamed the hills and deserts of the Land of Israel. Ostriches, Persian fallow deer, oryxes and Somali wild asses get reacquainted with their environment here before being released into the Negev's nature reserves.

Where the cone–shaped Negev funnels into the translucent deep blue waters of the Gulf of Aqaba we find the port and vacation city of Eilat. At Israel's southern tip, Eilat shares the northern shore of the Red Sea with its Jordanian neighbor Aqaba and its Egyptian neighbour Taba. These shores are world–renowned for their fabulous coral reefs, teeming with a fantastic and colored variety of marine life. Conscious of the delicacy of this unique ecosystem, Israel and her neighbors are taking the first, faltering steps to work together to protect the corals from the ravages of marine pollution and other damage.

We have traveled from the snowy crest of Mount Hermon in the far north, to tropical Eilat on the Red Sea. On our way, the timeworn Land—Ha'aretz—has re-

vealed to us only a fraction of the historical and religious sagas played out on its stage. History is still being played out here as Israel gropes for an accommodation with its neighbors that may yet put an end to decades of conflict. Seen in the perspective of centuries, this is sadly apt. The Land that inspired belief in one God and in universal values of law, justice and peace, has known little peace itself during its 5,000–year history. The sun sets dramatically over Eilat's granite hills, splashing ribbons of red and gold across the sky, igniting the senses.

The Holy Land, Palestine, Israel, has inspired the best and the worst in mankind, perhaps in equal measure. But there is a vitality to Israel that reverberates within the human spirit. It suggests that the land that was the moral compass of the past may yet hold the secret to a better future.

60-61 Coral Beach, Eilat. On the western flank of Israel's southernmost city the Negev becomes the Sinai Desert. The mountains in the background are in Egypt.

61 top A causeway allows divers and snorklers to enter the sea without trampling the delicate corals that are one of Eilat's main attractions.

61 bottom Eilat, hugging the northern tip of the Gulf of Aqaba, shares its airport with the adjacent Jordanian city of Aqaba—one example of regional cooperation that could spread in an era of peace.

61

62 The red–roofed Jewish neighborhoods of northern Jerusalem are largely populated by ultra–orthodox Jews.

63 Jaffa Gate, so named because the road leading from it ended in Jaffa. The walled Citadel in the center once contained the magnificent Palace of Herod but its ruins were erroneously identified by the Byzantines as David's Palace which is why the Mameluke tower on the battlements, a prominent symbol of Jerusalem, is referred to as David's Tower.

64–65 On Mount Zion,
the Church of the Dormition
of Mary and the tower of
the Dormition Abbey face
Christian cemeteries.
Suleiman the Magnificent's
architects were reportedly
executed for leaving Mount
Zion outside the rebuilt
ramparts.

65 Originally established as the Church of Constantine in the fourth century, the Church of the Holy Sepulcher marks the traditional site of the crucifixion, sepulcher and resurrection of Jesus. Today, prayers there are divided among six different Christian denominations: Greek Orthodox, Armenian, Roman Catholic, Syrian Orthodox, Coptic and Ethiopian.

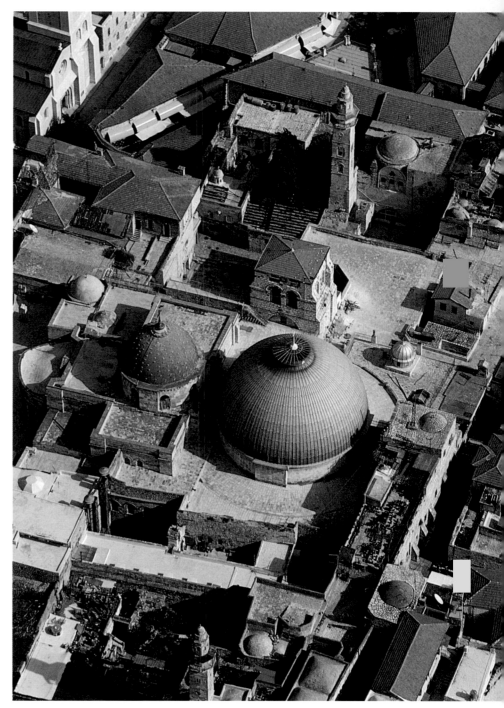

66–67 For religious Jews,
living inside the restored
Jewish Quarter is considered
a special privilege. The arch
at center right commemorates
the site of the Hurva
Synagogue originally built
in the thirteenth century
by the sage known as
The Ramban.

67 top The restored Batei Machaseh Square in the Jewish Quarter combines ancient and modern styles.

67 bottom Today, the Old City is linked to the New by landscaped gardens and modern roads, but still remains a world unto itself.

68–69 The Christian Quarter of the Old City is dotted with churches of different denominations. The large dome in the center is the Church of the Holy Sepulcher.

70 *The Temple Mount or Haram al Sharif is graced by the triumphant Dome of the Rock, which occupies the spot where King Solomon's Temple may have stood. The splendor of its exterior is matched only by its fabulous, ornate gold, red, white and green arabesque interior. The El Aqsa Mosque to the south is, however, the more important center for prayer.*

71 *The Dome of the Rock was built in 691–92, some fifty years after the first Arab conquest, as a shrine even to the Holy Rock believed to be the place of Mohammed's ascent to heaven. The dome was recently recovered with pure gold plates.*

72–73 *Haram al Sharif, its eastern and northern sides laid out with gardens, dominates the Old City with its majestic presence. The structure in front of the Dome of the Rock is the Dome of the Chain.*

74–75 The new Supreme Court, set in the Rose Garden, looks placid enough from above but has already been the scene of some hard–fought legal battles.

75 top Jerusalem is the seat of Israel's national institutions. The low rectangular building is the Knesset, Israel's parliament.

75 center Safra Square is the new home of Jerusalem Municipality. The old municipal building still carries the scars of the battles for control of Jerusalem.

75 bottom The Monastery of the Cross in the Valley of the Cross, thought to be the source of the cross on which Jesus was crucified.

76–77 Mea Shearim (One Hundred Gates) was among the earliest Jewish neighborhoods to develop outside the walls of the Old City. Its population is made up of ultra–orthodox Jews. In the mid–distance are the walls of the Old City at Damascus Gate.

78–79 A protected green area surrounded by dense residential neighborhoods, the Valley of the Cross encompasses the ancient and the modern: the Monastery of the Cross, the Israel Museum (center left), which houses many of Israel's archaeological and artistic treasures, and the pagoda–shaped Knesset.

80 top Dominus Flevit or "Our Lord Wept," half way down the Mount of Olives, recalls the tears of Jesus.

80 center The Seven Arches Hotel on the crest of the Mount of Olives is surrounded by the vast, ancient Jewish cemetery.

80 bottom Augusta Victoria, named after the German Empress, was built as a hostel and a hospital. Kaiser Wilhelm II paid a state visit to the Holy Land in 1898.

81 On top of the Mount of Olives facing the Old City to the west. The tower belongs to the Russian Monastery and the round building next to it is the Church of the Ascension.

82 *The Franciscan Church of the Visitation in the quaint village of Ein Karem on the outskirts of Jerusalem. Ein Karem is reputed to be the village where Mary visited Elizabeth.*

83 top *A general view of Ein Karem nestling in its valley.*

83 bottom *Mary's words to Elizabeth: "My soul magnifies the Lord and my spirit rejoices in God my Saviour" are recorded in fourty–one different languages inside the Church of the Visitation.*

84 top At Neot Kedumim on the outskirts of Jerusalem, a group of enthusiasts are employing ancient agricultural methods to recreate a biblical farm

84 center A train chugs along the Sorek Valley to Jerusalem, passing ancient terraces on its way.

84 bottom The capture of the Castel, a strategic Arab hilltop position on the road to Jerusalem, helped break the siege of Jerusalem in 1948. It is now a national monument.

85 Sha'ar Hagai, controlling the road between Tel Aviv and Jerusalem, was a strategic target in the struggle for the city in the 1948 War of Independence. Remains of destroyed armored vehicles line the road as a reminder.

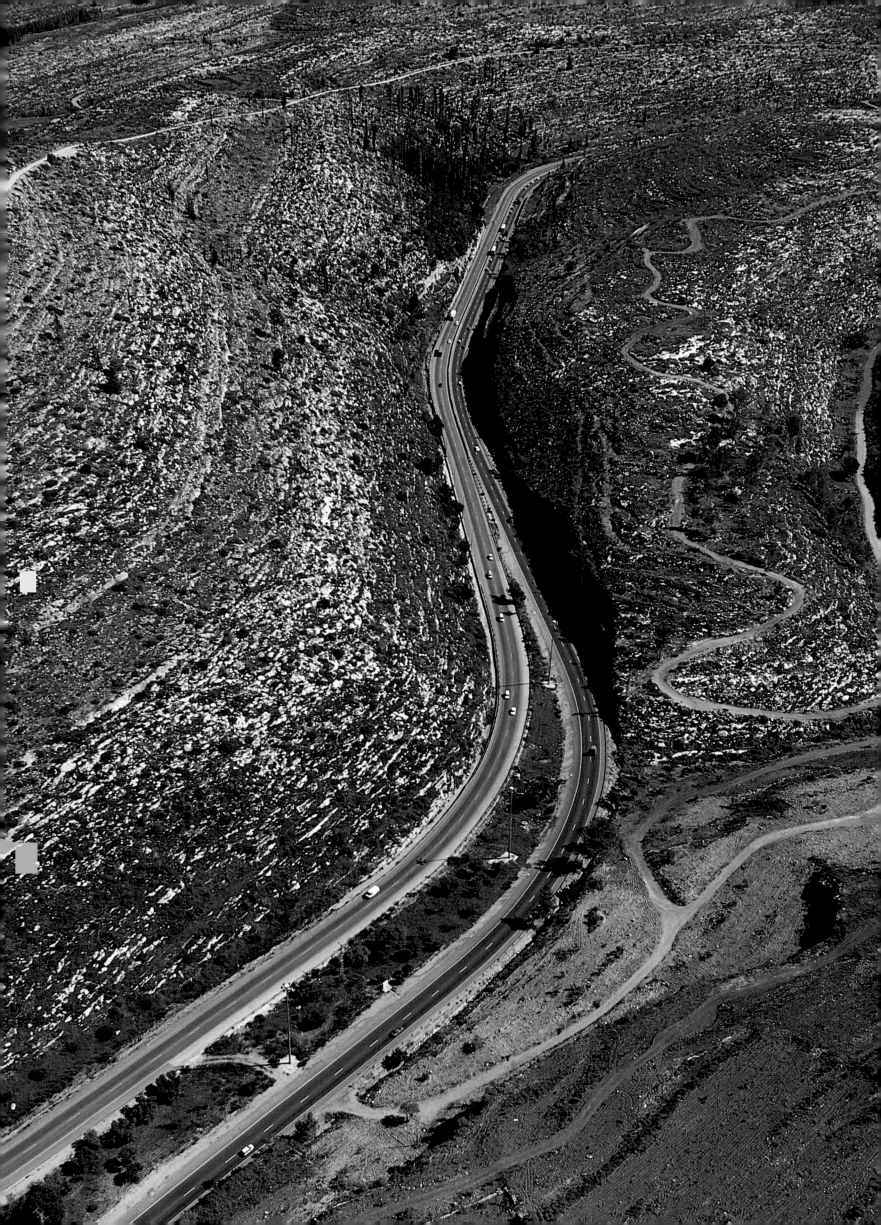

86–87 *The main road to Jerusalem. In the foreground is the Christian Arab village of Abu Ghosh, the venue of an annual festival of liturgical music.*

*87 top Har Hamenuchot,
at the entrance to Jerusalem,
is the city's modern
cemetery.*

*87 bottom Mevasseret Tzion
on the fringes of the Tel
Aviv–Jerusalem highway,
is a new dormitory town,
most of whose residents work
in the capital.*

88 *Like the Trappist Monastery, the Communité de Beatitude is situated near what is believed to be the site of Emmaus where the resurrected Jesus appeared before followers.*

88–89 *The Armored Corps Museum at Latroun in the Vale of Ayalon. Despite a series of determined attacks, Latroun held out against Jewish forces in 1948 but was captured in 1967.*

89 top *The beautiful Trappist Monastery at Latroun is a silent island in a sea of olive trees.*

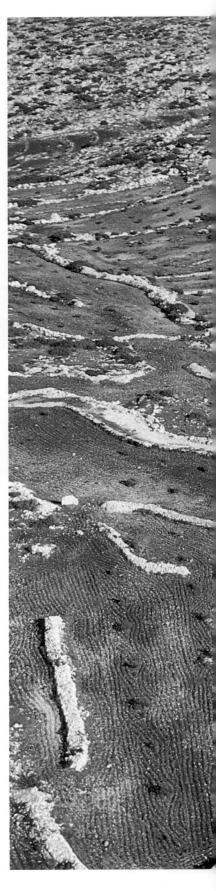

90 top and 90–91 Throughout the ages, the rocky slopes and hillsides have been cleared to make way for precious land that can be tilled and planted. The rocks are used to make stone walls that retain water and prevent erosion.

90 bottom These traditional flat–roofed houses, in a Palestinian hamlet near Hebron, are scattered among the villagers, terraced fields.

91 top *The Shepherds Fields near Bethlehem were once used for grazing sheep and goats. Three shrines in this area recall the story of the shepherds who saw the multitudes of angels proclaiming the birth of the Messiah (Luke 2).*

92–93 *The olive, valuable for its wood, fruit and oil, has always been a staple of the area.*

THE DEAD SEA
AND THE JUDEAN DESERT

94 The primordial
landscape of Nahal Pratzim
near the Dead Sea reveals
the ravages of wind and
water.

95 The monastery of St.
George of Koziba on the
perilous cliff face of Wadi
Qelt, was a center of the
ascetic monastic movement
that flourished in the Judean
desert after the adoption of
Christianity by the Roman
Empire in A.D. 324

96 The mosque of Nebi Samuel, traditionally identified as the resting place of the Prophet Samuel, was built over an older structure erected by the knights of the First Crusade.

96–97 According to Muslim tradition, Nebi Moussa (The Prophet Moses) is where Moses is buried. The site became a place of pilgrimage and a defensive position. The cemetery surrounding it belongs to the Bedouin tribes of the Judean Desert.

97 top The Jerusalem–Jericho road runs like a ribbon through the undulating hills of the Judean Desert.

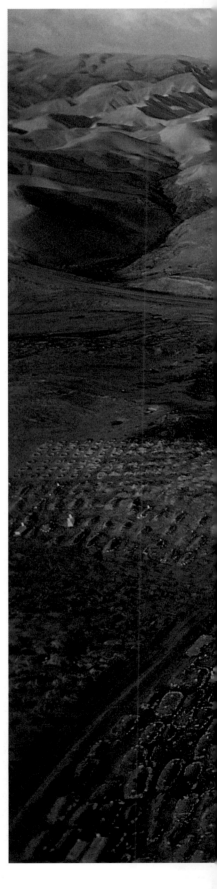

98–99 *The desert oasis of Jericho lies in the plain of the Jordan Valley as it enters the Dead Sea.*

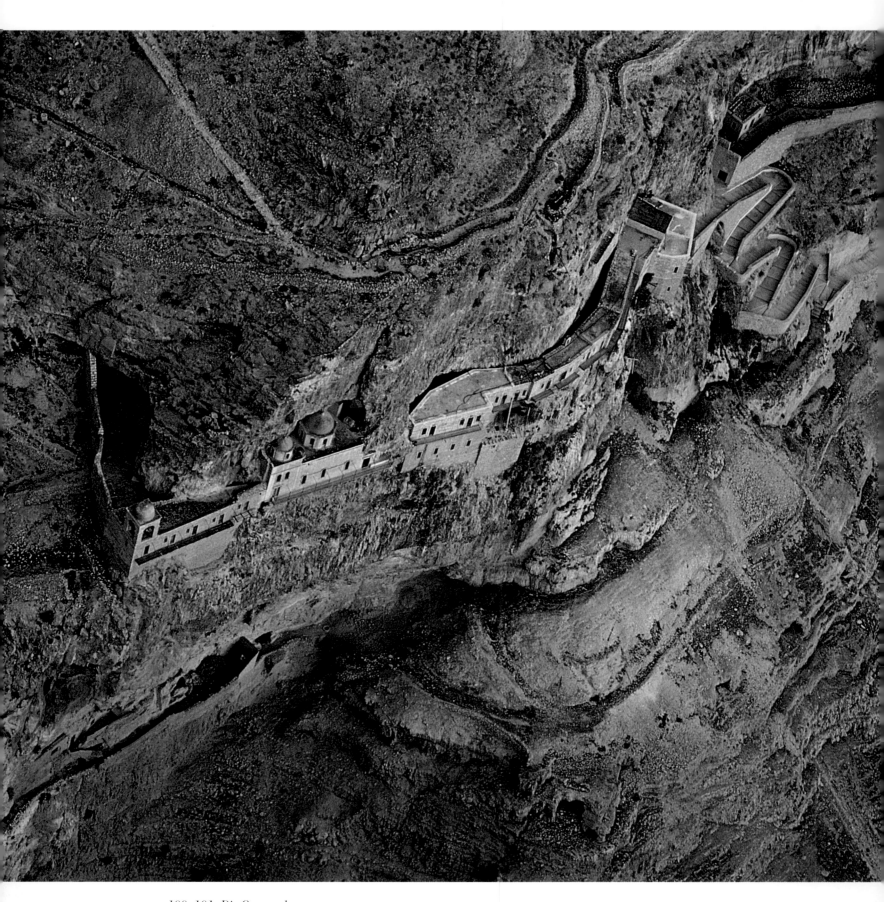

*100–101 Dir Qarantel, a
Greek Orthodox monastery
built on a mountainside west
of Jericho, is associated in
Christian tradition with the
Temptation of Christ.*

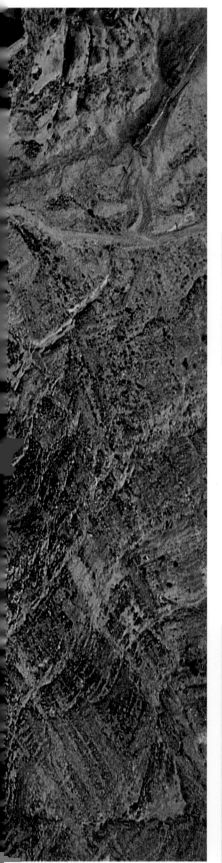

101 The monks who lived in caves near Dir Qarantel in Byzantine times established the original monastery on the mountain top. Work on the cliff–side buildings started in the Middle Ages.

102–103 In the eighth century, the rulers of the Arab Ummayad dynasty, attracted to Jericho by its warm winter climate and abundance of water, built this splendid winter palace, known as Hisham's Palace.

104 top Between the settlement and fields of Kibbbutz Ein Gedi, Nahal Arugot, a popular route for hikers, cuts into the mountains. An oasis inhabited since pre–history, Ein Gedi once guarded the recipe for a precious perfume made from persimmon.

104 bottom The cliffs above Ein Gedi with the eastern Jordanian coast of the Dead Sea in the background.

104–105 *The tongue of dry land jutting into the southern section of the Dead Sea creates one of the evaporation pools from which minerals are extracted.*

*106 The Dead Sea salt
pools, shimmering in the
heat, create abstract effects.
Potash, bromine, magnesium
and salt are drawn from the
Dead Sea in vast quantities.*

*107 The salt flats with
pillars of salt sticking out
of the evaporation pools.*

*108–109 The excavation
of salt and minerals is
transforming the landscape
of the southern Dead Sea.
The water level has dropped
dramatically over the past
few decades leading many
to fear for its future.*

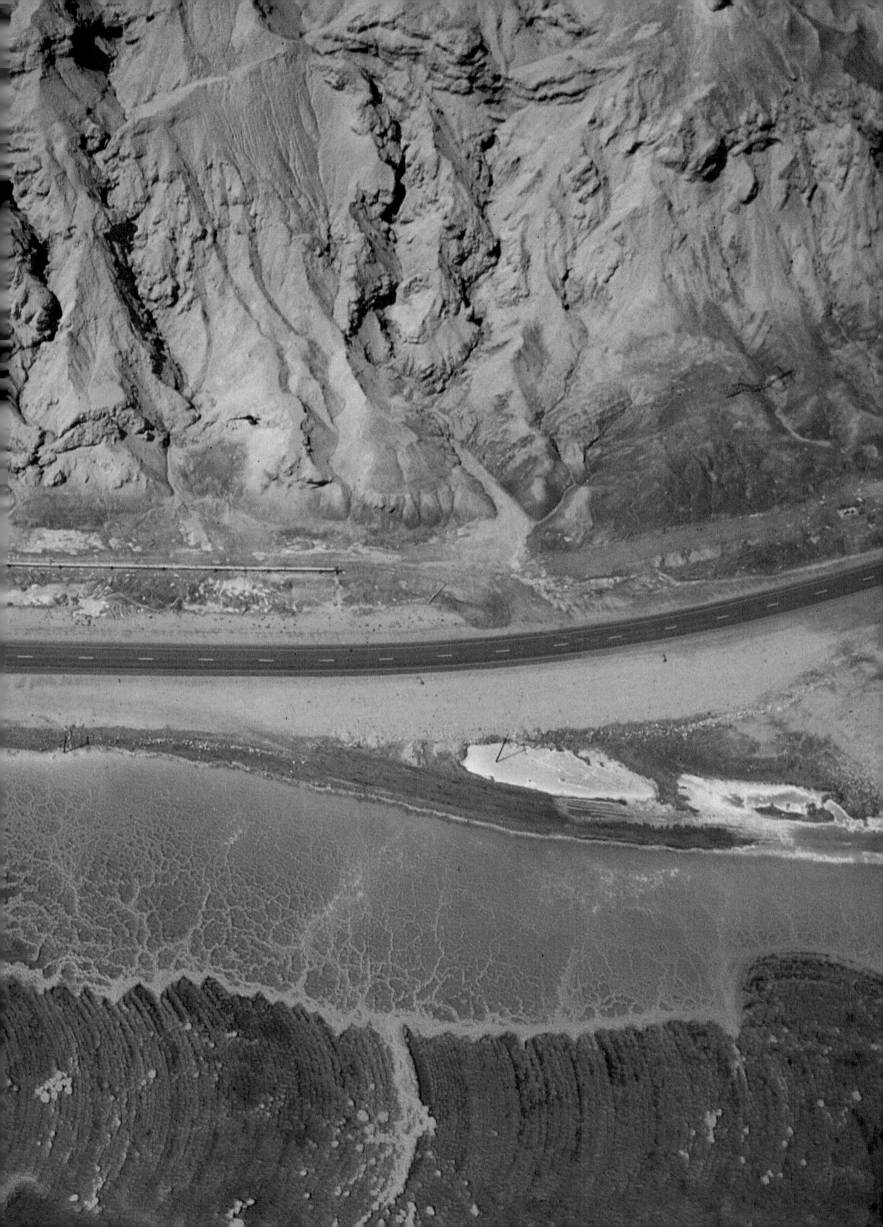

110 top and 110–111
The Moriah Hotel and the
beach at Ein Bokek. The
Dead Sea is a popular health
resort and its mineral, health
and beauty products are
marketed all over the world.

110 bottom The glorious
sensation of complete
buoyancy has to be
experienced to be believed.
Although it is impossible to
sink in the Dead Sea, drinking
the water is not advised.

111 top The hotels and
mineral spas of Ein Bokek –
the lowest holiday resort
on the face of the globe.

112–113 *The mineral rich, fissured earth is exposed by the receding water line.*

114–115 *The raw materials produced from the Dead Sea are laid out in front of the Dead Sea Works like a child's paint box.*

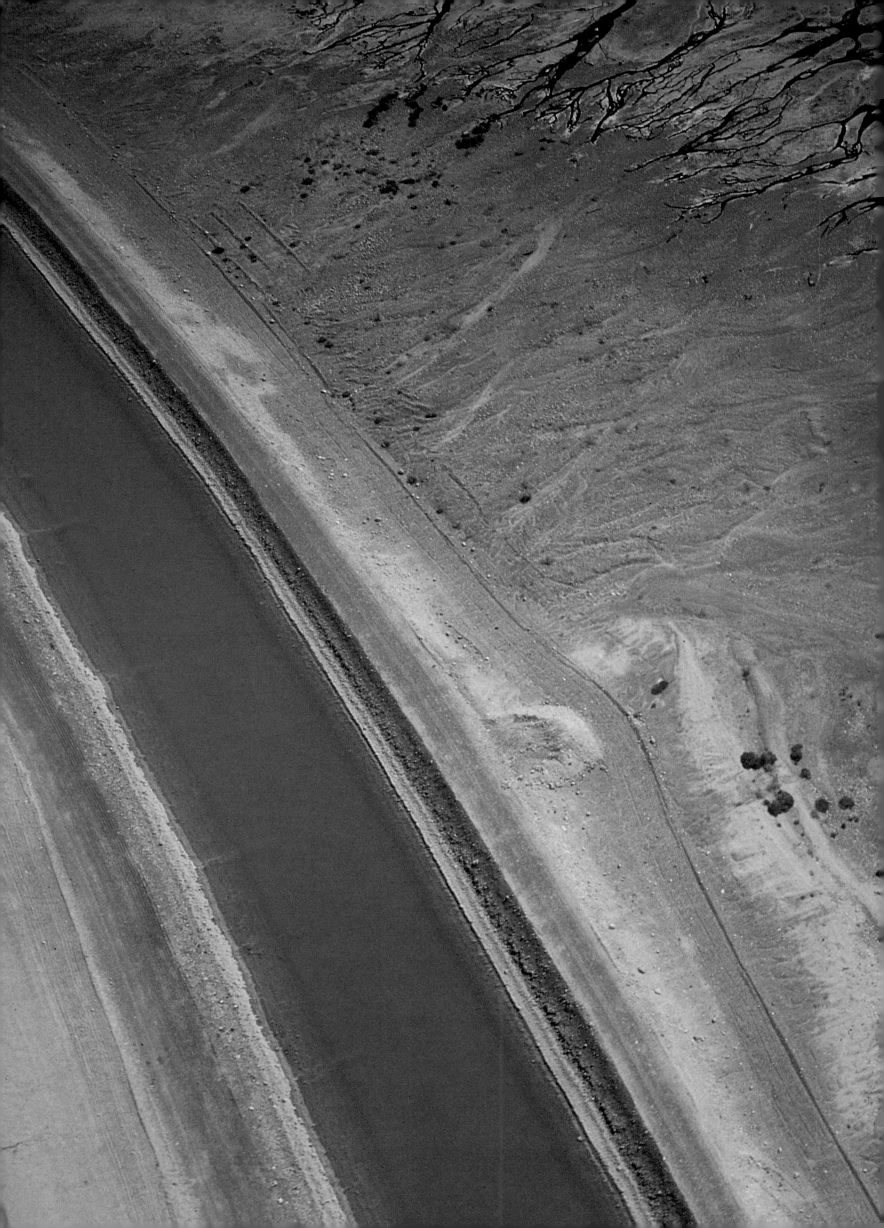

116 top The impregnable fortress of Masada was first occupied by the Hasmonean kings. In B.C. 40, Herod the Great left his family here while fleeing the forces of his Parthian rival Antigonus. After reclaiming his kingdom, he built an elaborate fortress and palace here. The upper platform was surrounded by casement walls with towers placed at strategic locations. A drainage system brought rain water from dams in the nearby wadis to twelve cisterns on the lower slopes, from where it was hauled up the steep and winding Snake Path by men or donkeys.

116–117 After Masada was seized in A.D. 66 by Jewish zealots in the First Revolt against Rome, the Roman general Flavius Silva and his Tenth Legion laid seige to it and finally succeeded in bursting through Herod's walls by building a huge ramp from which they could operate their battering rams.

117 With the help of his engineers, Herod added a triple–tiered hanging palace—used only for entertainment—to Masada's northern wall. The top level consisted of a round hall, the middle level was also round and carried a conical roof while the bottom level was rectangular and contained a bathhouse. All were linked by an outer, covered staircase. The Jewish rebels made many changes to Masada, adding, for example, two ritual baths.

118–119 According to the historian Josephus Flavius, in A.D. 73, their defenses finally breached, the last ten rebel leaders, having killed their families, cast lots to see who kill would kill the other nine before commiting suicide. Almost a thousand people perished at Masada.

120 top The largest of the Judean Desert monasteries—Mar Saba—hangs over a deep gorge in the Kidron Valley. It was founded in the middle of the fifth century by the monk Sabas, who had a powerful influence on the monastic movement.

120–121 Mar Saba was badly damaged in the Persian invasion of 614 but was later rebuilt and fortified. The bones of its founder, the monk Saint Sabas, were removed by the fleeing Crusaders and returned to the monastery only in 1965.

121 Despite its distinctive blue domes, Mar Saba seems to melt into the desert vastness when viewed from a distance.

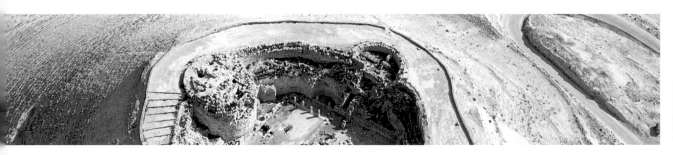

122 *The distinctive cone of Herodium, rising above the bare hills south of Jerusalem, can be seen from miles around.*

122–123 *Herod's magnificent palace, Herodium, was also intended to serve as his mausoleum. Placed on a natural hill and heightened by an artificial mound, the conical building, which included a large pool and luxurious living quarters, was guarded by massive circular towers.*

124–125 These "ships of the desert" loping across the barren wastes were once the main form of transport and are still highly prized by the Bedouin.

123

126 White–robed Christian pilgrims being baptised in the waters of the Jordan at the baptismal site of Yardenit. Nazareth, the area surrounding the Sea of Galilee and the banks of the Jordan, was the home of Jesus in his formative years.

127 In this section of Jordan, popular with whitewater rafters, the river twists and tumbles its way down to the Sea of Galilee.

128–129 Before it enters the Sea of Galilee, the River Jordan spreads rivulets into a swampy delta called Beit Tzeida, or Bettecha. In the fierce heat of summer, hikers can wade, chest deep, through the cool water.

130 At Beit Tzeida (Bettecha) the Jordan splits and enters the Sea of Galilee. Even at the height of the spring rains, the Jordan is never wider than about 40 yards and in summer it turns into a narrow stream that can be waded across easily at many points.

130–131 The farming village of Yavniel overlooks the southern tip of the Sea of Galilee, where the Jordan exits the lake and continues its path down the Jordan Valley. In the background are the cliffs of the southern Golan Heights.

*132–133 This view shows
the place where the Jordan
enters the Sea of Galilee.*

134–135 Tiberias, on the western banks of the Sea of Galilee, with Safed perched in the mountains in the background. Established by Herod Antipas, the son of Herod the Great, Tiberias was also an important centre for the Jewish People. Much of the Talmud, the book of laws and customs, was written here.

135 top Kibbutz Ginnosar with Tiberias in the background, set in the fertile Ginnosar Valley. The Jewish–Roman historian Josephus Flavius wrote: "For the whole area (of Galilee) is excellent for crops and pasture and rich trees of every kind, so that by its fertility it invites even those least inclined to work on the land."

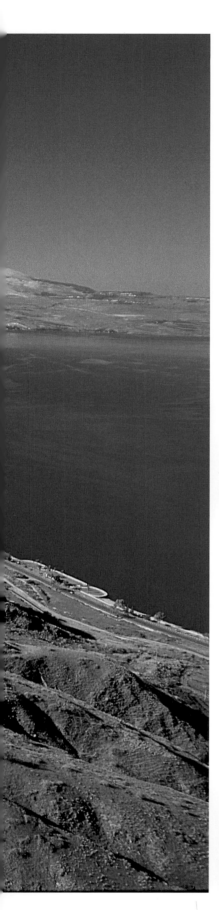

135 bottom The River Jordan slips out of the Sea of Galilee and into the Jordan Valley between the village of Kinneret and Kibbutz Degania. The snowy crest of Mount Hermon can be seen in the far distance.

136–137 The lakefront resort area of Tiberias adjoins the remains of the ancient walls that were rebuilt in 1833 during the rule of the Ottoman Governor Ibrahim Pasha. Herod

Antipas linked Tiberias to the older area of Hammat with its natural hot springs. An unusual fourth century synagogue mosaic displaying the signs of the zodiac has been found at Hammat.

138 top *The Mount of the Leap is considered by most Christian traditions to be the place, mentioned by Luke, where Jesus jumped from the mountain from the angry congregation* *he antagonized in the synagogue in Nazareth. It also commands an awesome view of the Jezreel Valley, from Mount Carmel in the west to Mount Tabor in the east.*

140–141 *The Franciscan Church on the Mount of Beatitudes where Jesus is reputed to have delivered the Sermon on the Mount. The remains of an early Christian shrine were found nearby and the entire area resonates with a sacred tranquillity.*

138–139 *Caves in the Arbel nature reserve overlooking Tiberias zone served as a place of refuge and habitation since prehistoric times. In the revolt against the Romans they provided an effective stronghold for the Jewish rebel forces.*

139 *The Eshkol Reservoir (top), in the Beit Netufa Valley of central Galilee, receives water pumped from the Sea of Galilee and carried by the National Water Carrier (bottom).*

142 top Capernaum, or Kfar Nahum as it is called in Hebrew, was the center of the Galilean ministry of Jesus. The octagonal roof in Capernaum covers the remains of a similarly shaped basilica built in the fifth century over what is traditionally considered to be the house of St. Peter.

142 bottom The Greek Orthodox Chapel at Capernaum was built among the seventh century remains of what was then a fishing village. At the time of Jesus, Capernaum was reputed to have had a population of more than 4,000 people.

142–143 *The white limestone synagogue pictured here was probably built at the end of the fourth century and must have contrasted with the black basalt buildings of the rest of this important center.*

144–145 and 145 top
Orchards in the Jordan Valley.
Although the climate is hot
and dry, careful irrigation
has turned some parts of
the Valley into a rich
agricultural land.

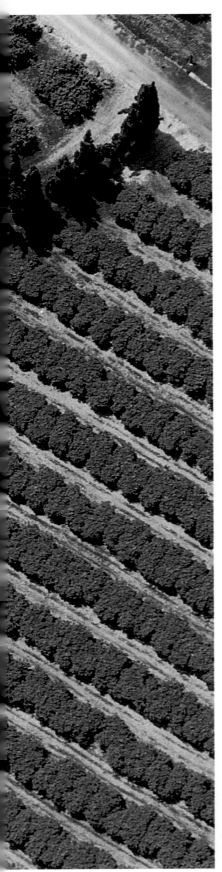

145 bottom Although Israelis are not great wine drinkers, the country has begun producing some prize–winning varieties.

146–147 The pattern of agriculture follows the natural topography. Trees planted in a wadi conserve the soil and also mark off different crops.

148–149 The patchwork fields of the Jezreel Valley. The trials and tribulations of the early Zionist pioneers have been vividly recorded in Israeli works of fiction, such as Meir Shalev's The Blue Mountain.

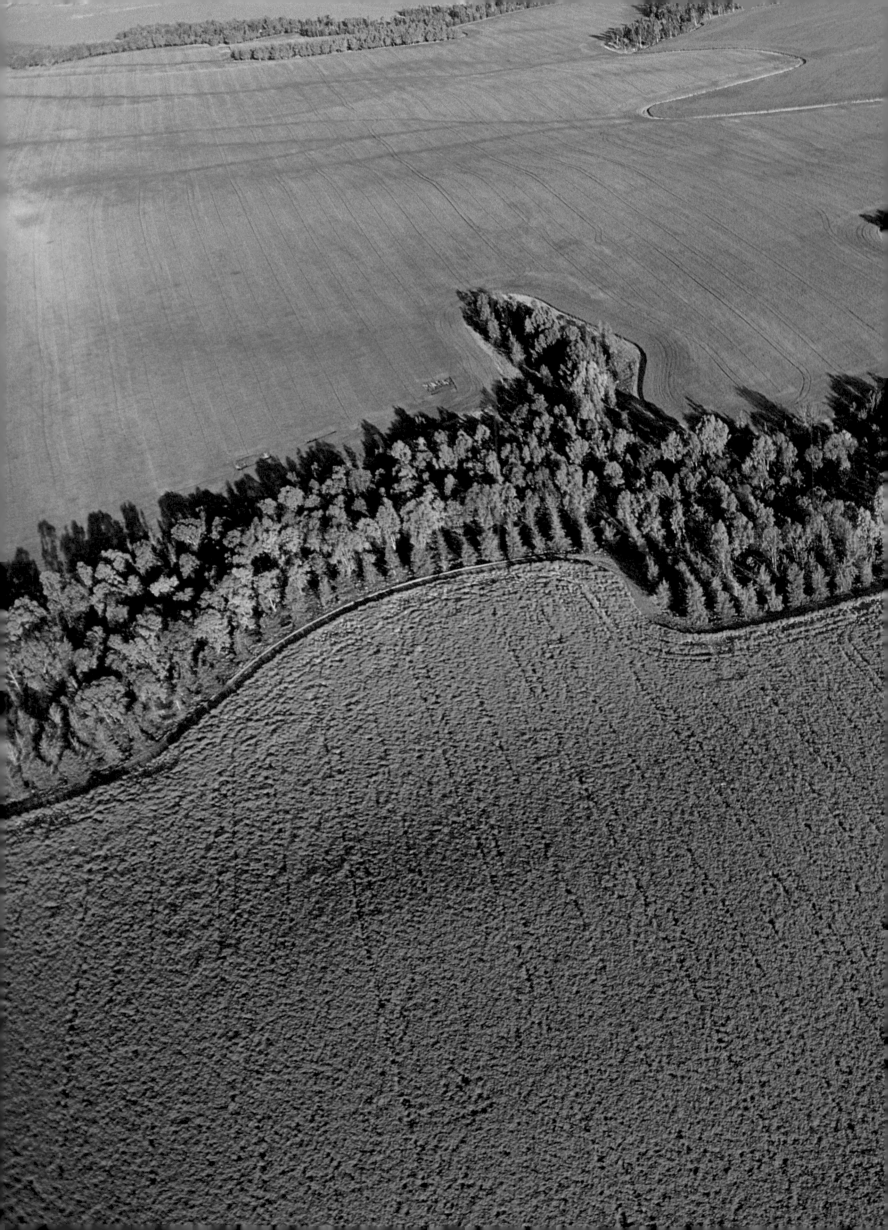

150 The aptly named
Belvoir (Fair View) Castle
with its commanding view
of the Jordan Valley was
built by the Crusader Knights
Hospitallers. Conquered by
Saladin in 1189, it was
dismantled in 1217 but
remains in a relatively
good state of preservation.

151 This section of the
extensive Cana'anite and
Israelite remains at Tel
Hatzor was built by King
Solomon and served the
succession of Israelite kings
who reigned in the first half
of the first century BC.

152 top The remains of Byzantine churches and Crusader fortifications lie within the gardens around the present Basilica of the Transfiguration built on Mount Tabor. In Jewish tradition, Mount Tabor is mentioned in connection with the war between the Jewish Prophetess Deborah and her Cana'anite rival Sissera.

152 bottom Rising distinctively from the valley floor, Mount Tabor is the Jezreel Valley's ultimate landmark.

153 The Basilica of the Transfiguration built on the crest of Mount Tabor marks the passage, in Matthew 17: 1–2, describing how Jesus took three disciples, "To a mountain alone and was transfigured, His face shining like the sun."

154 top The Basilica of the
Annunciation at Nazareth is
built over the traditional site
of the Annunciation by the
angel Gabriel to the virgin
Mary that she would bear
the Messiah (Luke 1). Built
over the remains of ancient
Nazareth homes, it envelops
the ruins of two earlier
churches.

*154 bottom A few miles
from Nazareth, the
Christian Arab village
of Kafar Kana is held
by many to be the biblical
site of Cana where Jesus
turned water into wine
at a wedding celebration.
A Franciscan church marks
the site of the miracle with
replicas of the six jars of
water.*

*154–155 Nazareth, the city of
the Annunciation, was a poor
village in the time of Jesus and
is now a bustling focal point
for the Galilee's Arab
population. The distinctive
watchtower of the Basilica
of the Annunciation, the most
famous of Nazareth's many
churches, can be seen near
the center. Mount Tabor
is in the left background.*

156–157 Megiddo, or Armageddon as it was later called, has a history going back to B.C. 3,300. Situated at a strategic point on the Via Maris trade route, it was a sacred site as well as an important fort and a major city. In Christian tradition, Armageddon (from the Hebrew Har Megiddo) is where the forces of Satan will meet the forces of Good at the end of days.

157 top The excavations at Megiddo have unearthed fourteen different layers of civilization and some of the findings have been hotly debated by archaeologists. The ruins pictured here include a round sacred area and a communal granary.

157 bottom This shaft leads to the long tunnel which channeled water into Megiddo from the spring outside the walls. Megiddo was where King Solomon built, "cities for his chariots and cities for his horsemen" (1 Kings 9:19).

158 The lake of Birket Ram in the northern Golan Heights is actually the crater of an ancient volcano. The Druse village of Mas'ada has grown up on its western banks.

158–159 Kibbutz Hagoshrim in the "Galilee Panhandle" also marks the northern edge of the Hulah Valley. The pool at adjacent Hurshat Tal, a popular picnic site, surrounded by 150 ancient oak trees, is fed by the River Dan, one of the sources of the River Jordan.

159 top Mount Gilboa viewed from the Jezreel Valley. After much of the Jezreel Valley was reclaimed from swamp it became an important center for pioneering settlement.

160 At the foot of Nimrod's Citadel lies the ancient city of Banias, named after the god of springs. A tenth century Muslim geographer wrote that Banias served as the bread–basket of Damascus. Some of the Crusader remains can be made out on the right.

160–161 Kla'at Nimrod (Nimrod's Citadel), which many researchers believe was first built by the Muslims, played an important role in the battles waged between the Crusaders and the Muslim armies in the twelfth and thirteenth centuries.

162–163 Now a part of the
Yehudiye Nature Reserve,
Gamla was an important
city during the period of the
Second Temple. Remains of
the earliest synagogue in the
Land have been found here.

163 top Rajum el Hiri or Ghosts Circle on the southern Golan Heights continues to puzzle archaeologists.

163 bottom The Golan Heights have been settled since pre–history and many sites have yet to be excavated.

164–165 The Hermon range exerts its commanding presence over the area. Sometimes, the snow at its peak remains well into the summer months. On the upper reaches, spring begins only in August, compared to March in the nearby Hulah Valley.

THE MEDITERRANEAN COAST

166 Natanya, with the hills of Samaria on the horizon. Environmentalists are warning that human tampering with the coastline, particularly the construction of marinas, will create irreversible ecological damage.

167 Israel's long, straight coastline, viewed here from the resort city of Natanya, stretches up to Achziv near the Lebanese border in the north.

168–169 Tel Aviv has much of the atmosphere of a European Mediterranean city, with free and easy ways and an appetite for the good life. Hot and humid in the summer, it is warm and pleasant in the winter.

169 top *The Tel Aviv Center for Performing Arts is the home of the New Israel Opera. Tel Aviv, almost a negative image of Jerusalem, is Israel's bastion of western–looking secular culture.*

169 bottom *The complex including the Mann Auditorium, home of the Israel Philharmonic Orchestra, and Habimah, Israel's National Theater, is one of the focal points of Tel Aviv's vibrant cultural life.*

170 top Tel Aviv's beaches, packed in the summer, are a jogger's delight in the winter months. The long, low Dan Hotel on the promenade must be one of the few hotels in the world to have been painted by an artist—again Ya'akov Agam.

170 bottom Dizengoff Center in the foreground is a city unto itself, containing a mall, cinemas, offices and residential areas, medical services and even a swimming pool. The "normality" of Tel Aviv, in a country often jolted by dramatic events, is considered one of its greatest assets.

170–171 The Israel Opera used to be housed in dilapidated premises, now replaced by the stepped "Opera Tower" on the right, which contains a shopping mall and a cinema complex. As the standard of living has soared, shopping habits have changed and air–conditioned malls are replacing corner shops.

172–173 The Yehoshua Park, in the north of Tel Aviv, is a vital green lung for hyperactive Tel Avivians. The skyline belongs to both Tel Aviv and adjacent Ramat Gan. Already a densely populated country, Israel is beginning to build upward in order to preserve open areas.

*174 top An interchange
feeds traffic into the big
city of Tel Aviv. Already
considered a developed
nation, Israel is experiencing
the dilemmas that come with
a rapidly changing society.*

*174 bottom The new marina
at Herzliya. Theodore Herzl,
the Austrian journalist and
founder of modern Zionism
from whom the city takes its
name, would probably be
pleased to note that some
Israelis can now afford their
own yacht.*

*175 The Ayalon freeway,
where Tel Aviv meets Ramat
Gan, is a restless intersection
for a country that seems
to be constantly on the move.
The office buildings house
the diamond exchange, once
a leading industry, now
being replaced by high–tech.*

176 The breakwater at Ashdod port cuts a swath into the deep blue Mediterranean. To the south lies the city of Ashkelon and beyond it the Gaza Strip.

176–177 Ancient Ashdod was one of the five main Philistine cities. Modern Ashdod, south of Tel Aviv, is Israel's second biggest port and an important commercial center.

177 top The influx of new immigrants from the former Soviet Union in the early 1990s has changed Ashdod's demography as well as its skyline.

*180–181 The outlines
of Herod's artificial port,
Sebastos, lie submerged
beneath the wharf built by
the Crusaders at Caesaria.
To the south, Herod built a
magnificent palace extending
into the sea. Caesaria was
built on the site of the former
Phoenician port of Straton's
Tower.*

181 top A large temple dedicated to the goddess Roma and the Emperor Augustus was constructed on a platform overlooking the port. This was replaced by a Christian church in the fourth century, when Caesaria reached its greatest size.

181 bottom The theater in the south of the city has been restored and is now an enchanting performance venue. Caesaria was built along classic Roman lines and also served as Herod's administrative headquarters, possibly in an attempt to counterbalance the influence of Jewish Jerusalem.

182–183 The raised aqueduct that brought water to the Caesaria from the Carmel range, on the horizon, was over five and a half miles long and was one of the most impressive in Palestine.

184–185 As can be seen from this new hotel that has sprung up on the sea front in Haifa, the city is trying hard to alter its image as a solid working town and to attract tourism.

185 top The tower atop Haifa University can be seen from all over the Galilee. Haifa is built on a series of hills, often affording a panoramic view of Haifa Bay.

185 bottom The sweeping view from the hotels on top of the smart Carmel neighborhood takes in the commercial and downtown areas, the busy port and the city of Acre on the far side of the bay.

186–187 The city where the Histadrut labor federation was born, Haifa is a pleasant, down-to-earth town. In the 1930's a large community of German Jews fleeing Nazism settled here and left their imprint on the cultural landscape. The Haifa Technion is Israel's leading technical university.

188 top This mosque on the lower slopes of Mount Carmel in Haifa is used by the city's Muslim population. Haifa is one the few cities where Jews and Arabs live side by side rather than in separate neighborhoods.

188–189 The Bahai World Center with its stupendous terraced gardens is the city's architectural pearl. The Bahai religion developed out of a mystical Islamic movement in the middle of the 19th century.

189 Set on a ridge, high above the commotion of the lower city, the smart Carmel neighbourhood is surrounded by green.

190 top If you take away the cars, the old city of Acre looks much the same today as it is did under Ottoman rule in the middle of the 18th century. The large building with the gray dome in the center is The White Mosque, which stands on the spot once occupied by the Cathedral of the Holy Cross.

190 bottom This Ottoman aqueduct, near the kibbutz of Lochamei Hagetaot, once carried water into Acre from nearby springs and remained in use until 1948. The kibbutz, dedicated to members of the Jewish resistance against the Nazis, contains a sobering Holocaust Museum.

190–191 On the other side of the bay, the Crusader ramparts of Acre jut out into the sea and seem to be entering a different time zone. Acre was always an important coastal city and was captured by a long succession of conquerors. The Crusaders renamed the port St. Jean d'Acre.

192–193 Laid out in gardens more reminiscent of the Palace of Versailles than of the Middle East, this Bahai site near Acre contains the grave of the Baha'Allah, after whom the Bahai faith is named.

191 top After being retaken from the Muslims in the Third Crusade of 1191, Acre remained in the hands of the Crusaders for an entire century. It was divided into quarters controlled by different orders of the Knights and the Italian city–states of Venice, Genoa and Pisa, which played an important part in defense and trade.

194–195 *After the city was taken from the Crusaders by the Mamelukes in 1291, Acre lay in ruins until it was rebuilt by the Bedouin–Ottoman ruler Dhaher el Omar and Jazzar Pasha who, in 1799, blocked Napoleon's advance northward.*

196–197 *Dor, with its small natural bay and lagoon, was a Phoenician port for centuries and remained in use until the 17th century* A.D. *In the sea off the coast, divers have found the remains of cannon and other weapons discarded by Napoleon's troops as they retreated from Acre.*

196 bottom The Crusader fortress in Atlit, south of Haifa, is named after the pilgrims who stopped on their way to help build it. After the fall of Acre in 1291 it was the last Crusader fortress to fall in the Holy Land. In the years leading to Israel's independence, Atlit beach was often used to bring "illegal" Jewish immigrants to Palestine.

197 top The beach at Michmoret, north of Natanya, forms a natural lagoon and is the site of a naval school.

197 bottom In the winter months, the fish ponds at the kibbutz of Ma'agan Michael are a favourite haunt of more than seventy species of migrating birds. Crocodiles lived in nearby Nahal Taninim until the end of the nineteenth century.

198 top The white cliffs and grottoes of Rosh Hanikra can be reached by cable car. In the third century, precious blue and purple dyes extracted from sea snails were made along this coast.

198 center The Rosh Hanikra promontory, also known as "The Ladder of Tyre" marks the northern border of the Land of Israel.

198 bottom Like too many of Israel's streams, Nahal Alexander, near the city of Hadera in the Sharon region, is now polluted and much of its former vegetation has been denuded. Efforts are underway to clean up the streams worst affected by pollution and to return them to their former natural state.

198–199 The coastline near Achziv in the far north becomes rockier as it approaches the Lebanese border. The banana plantations here almost touch the shore.

200–201 The national park
at the old port of Achziv is
a playground for campers
and divers. The big house
on the left was once declared
an "independent state"
and its eccentric owner even
produced passports for his
little plot of paradise.

202 The visitor center near the development of Mitzpe Ramon offers a stupendous view of the Ramon Crater.

203 Mount Ardon rises out of the lunar landscape of the Ramon Crater, the largest of three huge craters in the Negev highlands. These craters began as an anticline, or arch of stratified rock, whose weakened chalk and dolomite surface was eroded, exposing the even more vulnerable sandstone layers that broadened and deepened to form craters.

204 top With arable land being such a precious commodity in the Negev, every available plot is exploited–in this case the floor of a wadi.

204 bottom The kibbutz tractors have been careful to leave a ruined island intact. Most of the Negev's inhabitants live in the north of the region where there is enough rainfall to support agriculture.

204-205 These fields in the northern Negev belong to Kibbutz Dorot, where photographer Itamar Grinberg was born and grew up. The Patriarchs Abraham, Isaac and Jacob tended their flocks in the northern Negev, much as today's Bedouin do.

206-207 *Wadis and gullies continue to channel rock fragments out of the crater floor, which is over a thousand feet deeper than the surrounding cliffs.*

208-209 *Kibbutz Dorot hardly looks as though it* is situated in the middle of *a desert. Its main crops are garlic and carrots and it also produces sophisticated irrigation products. Most kibbutzim today combine agriculture with industry and other income producing branches such as tourism.*

210-211 *Farmers in the Lachish area of the northern Negev cultivate only the flat areas, leaving the hilly ground in its natural state.*

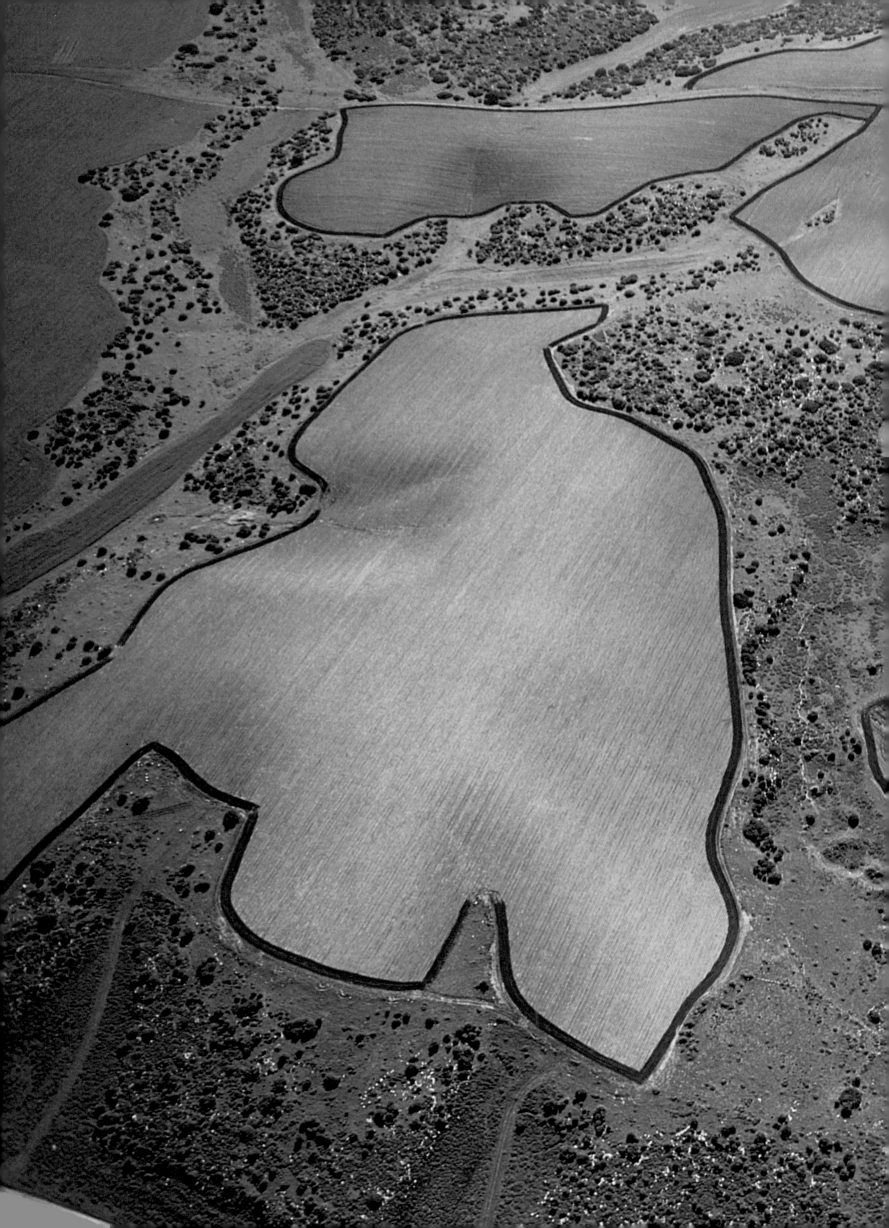

212 top The anticline arches of stratified rock are clearly evident on the walls of the Small Crater. The wadi exit in the center channels material out of the crater.

212-213 The flinty Etek cliffs near Timna, in the southern Negev, have withstood erosion better than their surroundings.

213 In the eastern part of Nahal Tzin, winter rainwater has penetrated the chalk to create a cool crevice that supports some vegetation. City dwellers take water for granted but finding it in the desert is a deeply joyful event.

214-215 Ma'ale Akrabim (Scorpions Ascent), part of the old road between Beersheba and Eilat, snakes its way up the mountain. Before the advent of air conditioning, taking a bus ride to Eilat was something of a challenge.

216 The artificial lake in the Timna Park seems somewhat incongruous in the rugged landscape. King Solomon exploited the copper mines at Timna, which were first used by the Egyptians.

216-217 This mushroom-shaped rock squatting in the barren Timna Valley is the result of thousands of years of erosion by wind and water.

218 top and 218-219
In some places, Nahal Tzin,
in the central Negev, opens
up into a broad valley.
In others, its water course
meanders around the slopes,
taking the route of least
resistance.

218 bottom A group of
tourists at an observation
point overlooking the
junction of the dry river beds
of Tzin and Akev.

220-221 Known to the Greeks as Mampsis, the first permanent settlement arose here at the end of the first century After Christ. One of the large, affluent houses discovered at Mamshit contains a wall painted in frescoes of Greek mythology.

220 top Mamshit was one of the cities on the Nabatean trade route that led from Eilat to Jerusalem via Hebron. Mamshit's gate was built during the Late Roman period and appears on the mosaic map of the Land of Israel at Madaba in Jordan as the symbol of the city.

220 bottom Avdat was another Nabatean way-station along the Spice Route between the Orient and the Mediterranean. Avdat reached its greatest heights of prosperity in the fourth to seventh centuries, during the Byzantine period, when the churches pictured here were constructed.

222-223 Remains of the Nabatean city of Shivta. The Nabateans learned how to utilize rainwater by channeling it into plastered cisterns. In the first century After Christ they lost control of the caravan trade and turned to permanent settlement, based on grazing and farming. After flourishing under Rome and the Byzantines, the Nabatean settlements were gradually deserted after the Arab conquest of 636.

*224-225 The fields of
Kibbutz Yotvata in the
Arava, the section of the
Jordan Valley leading to the
Red Sea. Incredibly enough,
Yotvata is famous for its milk
products. In the nearby Hai
Bar nature reserve, animals
mentioned in the Bible live
in a protected environment.*

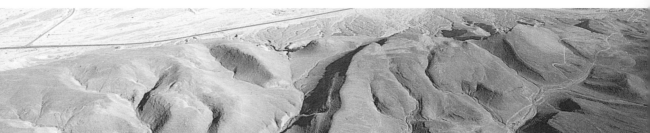

225 top Moshav Hatzeba in the Arava is a vivid example of how the desert has been made to blossom. Supplied with piped water from the north, it grows vegetables, melons and early Spring flowers for the markets of Europe.

225 bottom The Negev mountains meet the Arava, where fields can be more easily cultivated and irrigated on the flat valley floor.

226 *The northern beach of Eilat, its hotel area and marina. Eilat, with its year–round sunshine and coral reefs, is a popular destination for European winter sun-seekers.*

226-227 *The port and tourist resort of Eilat in the foreground gazes across the northern tip of the Red Sea at its Jordanian neighbor - Aqaba. Despite their proximity, until the 1994 peace treaty between Israel and Jordan, residents of Eilat and Aqaba were unable to visit each other.*

228-229 *Eilat's red granite mountains seem to dwarf the city. In the foreground, an artificial lagoon has been created to extend the beach area. Flights landing at the airport running through the middle of Eilat are gradually being transferred to Aqaba airport as regional cooperation gets underway.*

*230-231 At the Dolphin
Reef, visitors can cavort
with the friendliest mammals
on the face of the earth.*

231 *A tourist boat takes visitors for a trip around the bay where they can see flying fish and even the occasional shark. Glass-bottomed boats reveal the wonders of the coral reefs to non-swimmers.*

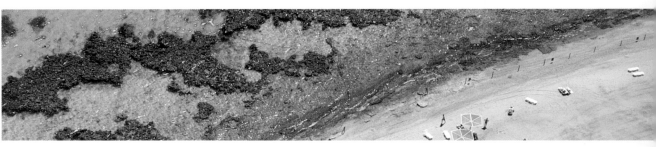

232-233 *Coral beach is a nature reserve where there are strict rules against fishing or damaging the corals. Conservationists warn that over development and pollution has already taken a toll on the reefs which, once damaged, take centuries to recover.*

234-235 *Paragliding across the deep blue waters of the Red Sea off Coral Beach. Water sports are an integral part of Eilat's lifestyle.*

*236 A hotel built after
the model of a Thai village
lies behind the underwater
observatory.
The observatory's circular
aquarium is an indoor coral
reef containing an amazing
collection of marine life.*

*237 The underwater
observatory allows visitors to
experience life under water
while remaining on dry land.
Moored alongside is the
Yellow Submarine, another
way of observing the
hundreds of species of coral
and some 1,000 species of
fantastically colored fish
that inhabit these clear
waters.*

*238-239 These two hotels
are separated by a spur in
the Eilat mountains as well
as by the Israeli–Egyptian
border at Taba. Plans are
underway to turn Eilat,
Aqaba and Taba into one
regional economic area.*

PHOTO CREDITS

All the pictures inside the book are by Itamar Grinberg, except for the following:

Marcello Bertinetti/Archivio White Star: pages. 1, 9, 11, 28-29, 29, 30-31, 31 bottom, 42, 43, 45, 47, 48 bottom, 50-51, 53, 65, 66-67, 67 top, 71, 75 bottom, 80 center, 97 top, 104 bottom, 121, 144-145, 145 top, 148-149, 173, 179, 198 bottom, 220 top, 220-221, 222-223, 225 bottom.

240 Agriculture has been central to the taming of the Land and the forging of its people.